The Guard of the Tree of Life, a Discourse on the Sacraments

By Samuel Bolton

The Guard of the Tree of Life, a Discourse on the Sacraments
By Samuel Bolton

Edited by C. Matthew McMahon and Therese B. McMahon
Transcribed by Josh Hicks

Changes made to this edition do not affect the overall language of the document, nor do they change the writer's intention. Spelling, grammar, and formatting changes have been made, and modernized wording is used in specific cases to help today's reader more fully grasp the intention of the author.

© 2012 by Puritan Publications and A Puritan's Mind

Published by Puritan Publications
A Ministry of A Puritan's Mind
4101 Coral Tree Circle #214
Coconut Creek, FL 33073
www.puritanpublications.com
www.apuritansmind.com
www.puritanshop.com

First Electronic Edition, 2012
First Modern Print Edition, 2012
Manufactured in the United States of America

eISBN: 978-1-938721-54-0
ISBN: 978-1-938721-55-7

TABLE OF CONTENTS

MEET SAMUEL BOLTON...5

[ORIGINAL TITLE PAGE] 7

PREFACE...8

A TABLE..12

A DISCOURSE ON THE SACRAMENTS................................18

The First Doctrine.. 22

Keeping the Heart.. 27

A Conscionable Use of Ordinances........................... 30

Exhortations 34

Meeting God.. 36

The Second Doctrine 39

Faith 46

Repentance.. 66

A Humble and Holy Reverence 72

Labor to See Fruit..75

Thankfulness 76

Obedience and Fruitfulness 78

Application of the Second Doctrine 85

The Third Doctrine..97

Reasons Why God Sanctifies Himself......................................99

Application 105

MEET SAMUEL BOLTON

Samuel Bolton, D.D. (1606-1654), divine and scholar, who has been wrongly identified both with a son and a brother of Robert Bolton, B.D., was born in London in 1606, and educated at Christ's College, Cambridge (Le Neve, *Fasti*, ed. Hanly, iii. 690, 607). In 1643 he was chosen one of the Westminster Assembly of divines. It is stated that he was successively minister of St. Martin's, Ludgate Street, of St. Saviour's, Southwark, and of St. Andrew's, Holborn. He was appointed, on the death of Dr. Bainbrigge in 1646, master of Christ's College, Cambridge, and served as vice-chancellor of the university in 1651. Although with "no ministerial charge" he "preached gratuitously every Lord's day for many years." It is believed that it was this Samuel Bolton who, in 1648, attended the Earl of Holland upon the scaffold (Whitelocke,

Mem. p. 387). He died, after a long illness on Oct. 15, 1654. In his will he gave orders that he was to be "interred as a private Christian, and not with the outward pomp of a doctor; because he hoped to rise in the day of judgment and appear before God, not as a doctor, but as an humble Christian." Dr. Edmund Calamy preached his funeral sermon.

His books are rare. They are: 1. "A Tossed Ship making for a Safe Harbour; or a Word in Season to a Sinking Kingdom," 1644. 2. "A Vindication of the Rights of the Law and the Liberties of Grace," 1646. 3. "The Arraignment of Error," 1646. 4. "The Sinfulness of Sin," 1646. 5. "The Guard of the Tree of Life," 1647. 6. "The Wedding Garment," and posthumously, 7. "The Dead Saint speaking to Saints and Sinners," (portrait prefixed).

For Further Study:

Brook's *Puritans*, iii. 223-4; Clark's *Lives*, pt. i. 43-7; Calamy's *Funeral Sermon*, 1654; Bolton's *Genealogical and Biographical*, Abram's *Blackburn*, p. 264.

[ORIGINAL TITLE PAGE]

THE

GUARD

OF THE

Tree of Life:

OR,

A Sacramental Discourse;

Showing
A Christian's 1) Privilege in approaching to God in ordinances;
2) Duty in his Sacramental approaches; 3) Danger if he does
not sanctify God in them.

BY SAMUEL BOLTON,

Preacher to the Congregation of *Savior's South-Wark.*

"Whosoever shall eat this bread and drink this cup of the Lord
unworthily, shall be guilty of the body and blood of the
Lord...He eateth and drinketh damnation to himself not
discerning the Lord's body," (1 Cor. 11:27, 29).

LONDON,
Printed by *G. Miller* for *A. Kembe,*
And to be sold at his shop at the *Talbot-gate* in *Southwark,* 1645.

PREFACE

TO MY BELOVED FRIENDS,

The godly and well affected of *Savior's-Southwark*;

Grace and Peace.

Beloved,

It is well-near four years since I was removed from a loving, a very loving people in the city, and fixed among you; the expresses of love which in this time I have received from you, have put me on to think, what way I might again manifest my engagements to you. And considering with myself the relation in which I stand, I could think of no better way of acknowledgment than to impart something spiritual to you; and no better subject than this which is not presented to your view, nor could I think of a better time than this for doing it, when God in our blood shows us what a fearful thing it is to be the guilty of the blood of his Son. It is not unknown to you how greatly this place above many others, has been guilty of the profaning of this *ordinance* of the Lord's Supper;

God has discovered it to us, humbled us for it, showed us the necessity, and graciously inclined your spirits to the desire of the reformation of it. In reference to which (through your countenance and assistance) my brother Minister and myself have adventured to set on the work, being willing to put yourselves to no little trouble, if by that we might prevent a great deal of sin.

In this work (the Searcher of hearts knows) we have had no other design than to express our Pastoral duties, and declare our Pastoral affections towards your souls. In short, we desire to serve you in love. Probably, we may meet with many obstacles in carrying on this work; indeed, it is that which is expected; no, and that which we reckoned on before we entered on it. But if the work is God's, he will either facilitate and make it easy for us, or give us spirits proportional to its greatness, I say he will either lessen the difficulties, or heighten our spirits to conflict and encounter with them.

There are two sorts of adversaries which we expect to meet with. Some that will say, we go too far, and others who will blame us that we go no further.

To them that think we have gone too far, I shall only say that we hope we have not gone beyond God's bounds. Sure as God has a purpose, this ordinance should be continued, so he has a care also, that it should be fenced from profanity in its continuance; and when a better way shall be discovered to us, in which we may hold up the use of this ordinance, and yet since it (in the use of it) from evident profanation, we are ready to listen to it, and be thankful for it. In the meantime, we do not see it our duty to hold up the use of this ordinance, except there are some since set up (all former senses being insufficient and now broken down) to keep this ordinance from manifest profanity, unless you will say our Pastoral office, in the exercise of it, necessitates us to sin. Much more might be said, if we saw it either requisite or convenient for an Epistle.

To those who blame us that we go no further, I must say our design has been rather to tempt on, by going their pace, than to discourage, by over-driving our little ones, I say it has been our aim to cherish, not to quench, to draw out, not to suppress the graces of our people, and therefore have we desired to improve those graces which we found, though weak, rather than to expect that which was not to be found. Our present Reformation is not the measure of our will, but of our power; it is not the utmost we desire, but the utmost we are able. And though it may seem small to you, yet do not despise the day of small things. Though the house is not built, yet we rejoice the first stone is laid, and we could not choose to bring it forth with shouting "Grace, Grace" to it, and "Glory, Glory" to the Lord. Babylon was not built in a day, neither is Zion; God carries on his works outside us, as he does his works within us, by degrees. The greatest fire was at first a spark, the tallest oak at the first an acorn, the strongest Christian had his infancy, and the greatest work of God its meager beginnings. Would the corruption of former times have suffered our godly predecessors, to have left the work in that forwardness to us, in which, through God's blessing, it may be left to them who shall succeed, possibly, no *probably*, the work might have been carried on to a greater height than now it can. That which is done we desire to bless God for it, and think it our duty to cherish with our utmost prayers and endeavors; in relation to which these ensuing sermons formerly preached, are now printed, to which work, if they shall be anything serviceable, they have obtained the end of him,

Who is not unwilling to spend and be spent for you,
Samuel Bolton.

A TABLE

A brief Table of the main things contained in the following discourse.

The Introduction into the Discourse and parts of the Text, and explanation of the term.

Doctrine 1: To have to do with an ordinance of God is to draw near to God.

1. Judge how much you are bound to God for ordinances.

2. What cause to lament the sad condition of those that lack them.

3. What a sin to disturb saints in the use of ordinances.

4. See the ground the saints so much taken with ordinances.

5. See what cause there is to keep our hearts in a holy frame.

Exhortation 1. To a conscionable use of ordinances on four grounds.

Exhortation 2. To conscionableness in the use of them on three grounds.

Exhortation 3. To exhort when you have to do with ordinances, take Christ with you.

The necessity of it: 1. In regard of admission; 2. assistance; and, 3. acceptance.

Doctrine 2. Those that have to do with God in an ordinance must sanctify God in it.

1. What it is to sanctify God in an ordinance.
    To which something is required.
        1. In the work.
        2. The workman.
            1. In his head, knowledge, *etc.*
            2. In his heart.
                1. Holy Affections.
                2. Suitable.
                3. Excited.

2. How we must sanctify God in this ordinance.
    1. Something is required before.
        1. Habitual.
            Preparation.
        2. Actual.
    2. Something in the time.
        1. Exercise of Grace.
            a. Faith.
            b. Repentance.
        2. Suitable Demeanor.
            1. Faith, where is discovered:
                1. What act of faith.
                2. On what object.
                3. For what benefits.

Faith is to be exercised for our benefits in the Sacrament:
    1. For the further assurance of our justification.
    2. For the increase of sanctification.
    3. For the subduing of corruptions.
    4. For deliverance out of temptation.

And his faith is to be acted upon Christ for these benefits, is discovered.

2. The second grace to be exercised in the time is Repentance.

    Where is set down:

        1. The kinds of mourning.

            1. Historical.

            2. Spiritual.

        2. The advantages of it.

            The discovery of love.

            The sufferings of Christ.

These are the Graces required in the time; now the demeanors.

    1. A humble reverence.

    2. Discharge of worldly thoughts.

    3. Something is required afterwards to sanctify God in this ordinance.

        a. Thankfulness and Obedience.

3. Why we must sanctify God. Three reasons.

    1. Because God commands.

    2. Because otherwise get no good.

    3. Because otherwise get hurt.

Use of Complaint.

    How few sanctify God in this ordinance.

Use: Examination; whether you have sanctified God in it before:

    1. See if you have observed God's order.

    2. See whether you observed God's rules.

    3. See whether you have observed God's ends.

    4. See if you have exercised God's graces in this time.

    5. See whether we have returned home with God's quickening and refreshments.

Doctrine. God will be sanctified of everyone that does not sanctify him in ordinances.

    1. What is meant by God's sanctifying himself on men.

    2. What are the reasons why God sanctifies himself on those who do not sanctify him in ordinances.

    Six reasons of it:

        1. For terror and dread of profane persons.

        2. For caution to others.

        3. To declare his justice.

        4. To remove scandal.

        5. To hold up his great name.

        6. To declare his hatred against sin.

Use: Caution to profane person's.

Use: To exhort us to turn our eyes backward, and examine whether we have not been guilty of the profaning of this ordinance.

The trial is put on three further designs.

    1. Sign: If the Sacraments have worked no further good on you.

    2. Sign: If you are worse after than before.

    3. Sign: If you have fed on nothing but outward elements, you have been a profaner of this ordinance.

A brief rehearsal and application of the whole to wicked and unregenerate persons.

IMPRIMATUR,

John Downam.

A DISCOURSE ON THE SACRAMENTS

"Then Moses said unto Aaron, This is that the Lord spake, saying, I will be sanctified in them that come nigh me," Leviticus 10:3.

We are all here present met together at an ordinance, and many of us have intended to go up a further ordinance. And there is no man or woman who has to do with any ordinance of God, but *has to deal with God* in it; he draws near to God. And God has said he will be *sanctified* in all them that *draw near* to him; either he will be sanctified by you, in your active glorifying of him, or on you, in your passive bearing his displeasure. There is never one of you here present, or any of you reading this treatise, but God will be sanctified and glorified in you this day. And it is my earnest desire that you may all actively glorify God, that he may not passively glorify himself on you, and raise his glory out of the ruins of any of you.

I do not need to travel far back to find you a coherence, the verse before will afford it; and the first word of my text bids me to go no further.

There is, 1. The occasion of these words. 2. The Preface to them. 3. The words themselves. 4. The effect of them.

1. The occasion of these words, and that was the untimely death of Aaron's two sons; their death gave birth to these words. And a sentence it is not too dear if bought with the lives of thousands of men. 2. The *preface* to them, *this is that the Lord said*; why, where did the Lord speak it? Did he speak it to Moses only? Or did he speak it to the congregation also? We never read it was written before, *totidem verbis (in the number of words)*. Some think this punishment was all the command they had, but I cannot think that God first punishes, and there on it raise a precept, but he first gives his Law, and then punishes its breach.

The words declare there had been some charge given; *This is that the Lord said*, so that there was some charge. But where was it? We do not read of it here. Some say it was spoken, but not written; and this they would have to countenance their unwritten traditions. Some will have it in Exodus 19:22, "Let the Priests sanctify themselves, lest the Lord break in upon them." Others will have it in Leviticus 8:35-36, "Keep the Lord's charge that you die not." Calvin will not have it referred to any particular place, but a general charge, given at diverse times, and now the present occasion brings it forth to particular application, to which I assent and agree. 3. We have the words themselves, *I will be sanctified.* Why, what is that? Can God be sanctified of us? Indeed he sanctifies us, but how can *we* sanctify him?

God is sanctified in two ways: *actively* and *passively.*

1. Actively, as 1 Peter 3:15, "Sanctify the Lord in your hearts," and so God is sanctified when we cherish and maintain high esteem of God in our hearts, when we honor, esteem, and advance God in our hearts and in our lives.

2. Passively, by punishing offenders, "When I have executed my judgment on her, then shall I be sanctified in her" (Ezek. 28:22). Jerome on this place says, "The punishment of offenders is the sanctification of God."[1] So you see it was in the text, God was sanctified on them, not by their doing good, but by their suffering evil; not actively but passively. And in both these senses the words are to be read, I say the words are to be read in this disjunctive sense, "I will be sanctified of all them that draw near to me;" that is, either actively, in glorifying me in the work; or passively, in glorifying myself upon the workman; if you do not sanctify God in an ordinance, he will be sanctified on you.[2] 4. We have the effect of these words on Aaron, it is said, "it struck him dumb;" a dutiful dumbness. He was silent to Jehovah, he held his peace;

---

[1] *Sanctificatio Dei offpaena pecantrium.* Jerome.
[2] *Si voluntas Dei non fiat a re, fiet de re.* Augustine.

he was dumb, and did not open his mouth because it was God's doing. God's will being manifest, it chained up his tongue, he held his peace, by it confessing, says Calvin, "That they were slain by the just judgment of God."[3] His silence cleared God in his dealings. And what a power is there then in faith, and grace, to silence the soul in such a sad condition as this? The loss of his sons, his eldest sons, when young, and without posterity, in the first day of their ministration, in the sight of the entire congregation, and by so fearful a judgment, fire from the Lord, and in the act of their sin, which some think was joined with drunkenness too, on which the prohibition against wine follows in verse 9 so that the congregation might suspect they went but from fire to fire, from a destruction by fire, to a preservation in fire, from a temporal, to an eternal burning? Yet in all this Moses having declared the author, God, the cause, their sin, so Aaron was dumb, and *held his peace*. It was not such a dumbness as Zachariah had, that was penal, and unbelief struck him dumb so that he could not talk. This was a spiritual dumbness, and faith struck him dumb. It did not so much suspend his tongue from speaking, as silence his heart from complaining and made him quietly submit to God's dealing.

---

[3] *Silet auditavourate Dei. Calvin. Justo Dei judicio exrinctos esse.*

THE FIRST DOCTRINE

So having at once shown you both the parts of the text, and cleared whatever had any appearing difficulty in it, we will now lay down the several conclusions the text affords us.

1. *That they who have anything to do with any ordinance of God, draw near to God.*

2. *That they who draw near to God in any ordinance, must sanctify God in it.*

3. *That if we do not sanctify God in an ordinance, he will be sanctified on us.*

We will speak a little of the first, which is an introduction to those which follow.

That they who have to do with an ordinance of God, draw near to God.

You see it is the language of the Spirit of God here, that to have to do with any matter which concerns the worship and service of God is, "to draw near to God." And in other places it is called "a coming before God, a treading his courts, and approaching to God, a meeting of God;" all which language imply this, that whoever has anything to do with God in any ordinance, do in fact draw near to God. You tread his courts, you come into his presence, you approach to God, you meet God, you have communion with God; no, you have to do with God's name. God's ordinances are part of his name. No, you have to do with God *himself*. He that has to do with any ordinance, with any part of his worship, has to do with God himself. When you have to do with the Word, when you go to prayer, when you have to do with sacraments, you have to do with *God himself in them*. What could the word do, either in commands to engage us, in promises to comfort us, in threatening's to terrify us, if we had nothing to do with God in them? What were prayers, but a distracted seriousness, a religious madness, if we had not to deal with God in it? What were the sacraments, but gaudy pageants, no, empty fantasies, beggarly elements, if we did not have to deal with God in them?

It is God that we have to deal with in ordinances, that sheds a glory, casts majesty, and puts an efficacy into all the ordinances we have to deal with. It is he who makes the promises of the Word rocks to stay and support that makes the commands of the Word full of authority that makes the threatening's of the Word exceeding terrible. It is he that we have to deal with, that makes a little handful of water, a little bit of bread, and cup of wine, exceeding glorious and efficacious. What empty, what poor, what contemptible things would these be (and are to unbelieving men) if we had nothing to do with God in them? It is this God we have to do with, that casts majesty on, and puts an efficacy into *every ordinance*.

But we will pass over this. If they, who have to do with any ordinance of God, draw near to God, then let me put some things to you in order to judge this rightly.

1. Judge then, if ever a Kingdom was more engaged to God than ours, who enjoys the ordinances by which we draw near to God. Has he dealt this way with any nation? What nation under heaven that enjoys the same privileges of drawing near to God in ordinances as we do? Well may we say in the words of the Psalmist, "Blessed is the nation which thou choosest, and causest to approach unto thee, that they may dwell in thy courts, we shall be satisfied with the goodness of thy house, even of thy holy temple," (Psalm 65:5).

2. And with blessing God for our own privileges, judge what cause we have to take up a lamentation for them that never enjoyed drawing near to God; and for them who have enjoyed, but are now *deprived* of this means of drawing near to God.

1. Them who never enjoyed the ordinances, who sit in darkness, and in the shadow of death, who never had a Christ, a Gospel discovered to them. O, pity and pray for them, that

the Word of the Lord might run and be glorified, that God would enlarge the bounds of his sanctuary, stretch forth the curtains of his Tabernacle, that the eyes of nations might be opened, that the fullness of the Gentiles might be brought in, and that they might flee to the Church as "doves into the windows," which is prophesied (Isa. 60:8). And with them, O remember that ancient nation, the Jews, who have drawn near to God in ordinances, but now at distance with him, and even set at further distance, by the use of those ordinances, by the use of those ordinance, by which formerly they drew near. O! remember them that blood which they imprecated on themselves for a curse, may now be on them for a blessing, that it may lie no longer on their heads, but now be sprinkled upon their hearts, and be in *venidam* (*pardon*), which has been so long in *vindictam* (*revenge*); that as it was said of the Gentiles, so it may now be said of the Jews, "That unto them is granted repentance to life."

2. And take up mourning for them who have enjoyed the ordinances, but now lack them. Look into Germany, look into Ireland, no, look into many places in England, how many Pastors, who are driven away from their flocks, how many Shepherds smitten, and the sheep scattered? How many poor scattered flocks, who had the manna fall at their tent doors, and their tents about the Tabernacle, who now have the

Tabernacle removed, are without Word, without sacraments, without ordinances, and are forced to wander from place to place, to gather of the bread of heaven, to enjoy the ordinances by which they may draw near to God?

3. Judge then, if it is not a vile thing to hinder and disturb the saints in those things, by which they draw near to God. 1. Either by depriving them of ordinances and robbing them of the means. 2. Or by corrupting of the ordinances to them, that they cannot enjoy them in that purity which God left them. In the first, the break is taken from them. In the second, they give them poison with their bread; both these will have a sad day of reckoning.

4. See what is the reason the saints are so much taken with ordinances, because they draw near to God in them; they look on ordinances as bridges to give them a passage to God, as beats to convey them into the heart of Christ (*vebicula spiritus*), as means to bring them into more intimate communion with their Father, therefore they are so much taken with them. When they go to the Word, they go as one goes to hear news of a friend; when they go to pray, they go to talk with a friend; when to read, they go to read a letter from a friend; when to receive, they go to sup with a friend. They look on ordinances as those things by which they have to do with God, and therefore are ordinances so precious. Indeed to

them who have to do with nothing but duty, in duty, but prayer, in prayer, but hearing, in hearing, to them the ordinances are dead, dry, and spiritless things; but they who have to do with God in duty, they have communion with God in ordinances, to them ordinances are passing sweet and precious.

5. Judge what cause there is to keep our hearts in a spiritual and holy frame; we have often to do with ordinances, and when we have to do with ordinances, we have to do with God, we draw near to him. And therefore, what cause to get and keep our hearts in a holy temper that we may be ever fit to close with God in them, and not have our hearts like bad servants, to seek when we are to use them. The Apostle bids us to pray continually. This is not meant that we are ever to be on our knees, ever in actual prayer, but seeing we are to pray so frequently, we are to get and keep our hearts in such a habitual frame and disposition, that they may be ever fit to close with God, whenever we are called out on the duty.

KEEPING THE HEART

Were we but seldom to have to do with God, you might think there were no such need of keeping our hearts in frame; but seeing we are to do with him daily, who is so pure and holy a God, "O, what manner of persons ought we to be?" How exactly should we walk? "Will you steal, and murder, and come and stand before me, in this house which is called by my name, saith the Lord?" (Jer. 7:9-10). So will you walk loosely, live vainly, when you are to do with so holy a God every day? O, let ever man that "calls on the name of the Lord, depart from iniquity." Let everyone that holds up praying duties, keep his heart in a praying frame; such a Christian is not worth a penny, who is only good when he is on his knees, who think it sufficient to snatch up affections to serve the turn of a duty, and then to lay them aside as soon as the duty is over; he is a Christian indeed, who prays on his feet as well as on his knees, whose life is nothing else but a real prayer; that if you look into his heart, there is all his desires engraved; his heart ever pants and breathes the same things he prays? And if you look into his life, his life speaks the same language his lips do; his life is a walking prayer, many men are one on their knees, another on their feet, but he is the same, he walks with the same spirit, the same affections, the same desires and disposition; he is the same man. It is something to pray, more to pray as a Christian, and more when you have prayed your prayers, to live your prayers; no, to live those affections, those dispositions where with you prayed, to live as high as prayer. It is a shame to see, how we slide out of duty into the world, and out of the world into duty again; as if we were two contrary men, one on our knees, and another on our feet. And therefore you shall see men to gather up some affections, some dispositions before they enter on a duty, and put themselves into another frame; but lay them aside as soon as ever they have done, these must only serve to act a praying part, when that is done, then lay them aside; you have no more use of them, you must put on another spirit to go into the world with. Christians, you have often to do with ordinances, and had therefore need to keep your hearts in an ordinance frame. He, who does not keep close to God in practice, shall never keep close to God in prayer; distance in life breeds distance in duty. And what need of keeping up praying affections? What shames to have our lives give our lips the lie, our practice be a confutation of our prayers? In our prayer to be warm, in our practice cold, up in duty, down in life? O learn to live as high as duty; you never pray indeed, until you practice come up as high as your prayers, until you love confessions and are humble, you love petitions and are thirsty, and diligent for those things you beg, until a man may read by your life that you are one who desire those things, which you have uttered with you lips. Let this frame of spirit be in your eye to aim at, and in your life to endeavor after. But I am talking too much here. I intended this doctrine only for the porch or entrance to the rest of the work, so let me therefore draw up the conclusion of it.

A CONSCIONABLE USE OF ORDINANCES

1. If it is so, that whosoever has to do with an ordinance has to do with God in it, he draws near to God; let them then exhort you:

1. To a conscionable use of ordinances.

2. To a conscionableness in their use.

1. Let me exhort you to a conscionable use of ordinances. Be more frequent in hearing, in praying, in receiving, *etc.* I might say something to this last, *viz.* receiving. The Apostle tells us, "As often as we eat this bread, we show forth the Lord's death," (1 Cor. 11:26); it implies a frequent use of the ordinance, more than once or twice a year, or once a quarter. Indeed the opportunities might be more frequent, if it were not for the coldness and deadness of our hearts. In the primitive times of the Church, while the blood of Christ was warm, they had the sacrament every day; we have an uncontradicted authority, that they had it every Lord's Day. And as men grew colder, so the distances grew greater. Sure, were it not for the coldness and deadness of our hearts, it might almost be our daily bread; at least we might enjoy a

more frequent use of this ordinance than we do. But as the Apostle says, "As often as you have opportunity, do good." So as often as you have the opportunity, take the occasions to meet God in his ordinances.

1. By them you see you draw near to God, you come into his presence, you have something to do with God's name; no, you have something to do with God himself.

2. By them God draws near *to you*, he walks among the candlesticks, he presents himself in his ordinances (Matt. 28:1) and there he directs us to find him (Song. 1:7-8).

3. If we do not keep up a conscionable use of ordinances, distance will grow between God and you. As the waterman may lose more by the omission of one stroke than he is able to recover again by man; so may you lose more by the omission of one duty, than you are able to recover again by the performance of many, especially, if this omission has arisen, 1. From neglect of God; 2. From carelessness; 3. From flighting of the converses with God; 4. Or from the importunities and solicitations of Satan and our corruptions; 5. Or from the brandishements of the world. If on such grounds, little do you know what you lose by such an omission. If not withstanding all endeavors, it is so hard to keep communion with God, what would it be, if we should cast up our oars and neglect it wholly? You see what a

distance was bred between God and Israel (Jer. 2). And what was the ground of it? "Why," says the text, "My people have forgotten my days without number," they had no care to keep and cherish communion and acquaintance with him, and so distances were bred between God and them. Neglect of duty breeds *strangeness*, strangeness *distance*, distance *falling off*. A good caveat in these days, when so many do cry down duty; shall we look on that as our burden which is our glory, our bondage which is our privilege? What is the happiness of a glorified saint, but only that he is always under the line of love, ever in the contemplation and converses with God? And shall that be thought our burden here, which is our glory hereafter? By this, first, you come to see the face of God; secondly, you have conversations with him; thirdly, you get new quickening's; fourthly, new encouragements; fifthly, fresh strength against sin; sixthly, new supplies against the temptations of Satan and the world; seventhly, fresh strength to walk with God; eighthly, armor against our lusts; and this is enough to make us conscionable.

4. We do not know how soon we may be deprived of ordinances; we have played with fire and God might put them on us, we have sinned in the light and God might put out our light. How justly might God remove his candlesticks, or let out his vineyard to other husbandmen, and seek for other

ground to sow the seed of his ordinances on, seeing the ground where it has been sown has brought forth so little fruit? How deserved might he suffer us to wish and wander to enjoy one of the days of the Son of Man which we have enjoyed?

But though God does not take away the ordinances from us, yet he may take us from the ordinances, and that not only by death, but in life itself, and a sad thought this will bring to your soul, when conscience shall report to you, your former negligence in the use of ordinances.

2. Let me exhort you not only to a conscionable use of ordinances, but to a conscionableness in the use of them; be not only conscionable to use them, but let your hearts be wrought up to a conscionableness in the use of them. The power of the Word, the terror of the Law, the fear of wrath, and the hope of reward may put a man to do duty, yes, and have power on the spirit, and engage the conscience to do duty. You see many that dare not but pray, and yet have no heart in prayer; they have a conscience to do duty, but their hearts are not brought to any conscientiousness in the doing of it. A common work of God may make men conscionable to do many duties, but nothing but the Spirit and grace of Christ will work up the heart to a conscionableness in the doing of them.

EXHORTATIONS

To this conscionableness in the performance of ordinances, would I exhort you on this ground, because you draw near to God and have something to do with him. And as in all ordinances this is so, it is true also in particular in this ordinance of the Lord's Supper.

1. Because otherwise you get no good: 1.) No good of grace, no improvement of holiness. 2.) Nor no good of comfort. Comfort does not come in from the bare doing of the duty, but from the *manner* of doing, it is not the issue of conscience to do, but of conscionableness in the doing of them. All the sermons you have heard, all the prayers you have prayed, all the sacraments you have received, though done out of conscience as you say, will not minister one drop of true comfort to you on your deathbeds if your spirits have not been wrought up to a conscionableness in doing them rightly.

2.) Because otherwise you provoke God; to give him the carcass and outside of duty, and to withhold the life and spirit of duty is a provocation of God.

3. Because otherwise you will contract much guilt, and bring much evil on your own souls. This is sure, that ordinances used in an unconscionable way: 1. They give Satan further possession of us. 2. They put much weight to our sin.

3. They set our souls at further distance with God. 4. They ripen us to the great downfall, the great sin lies among such. 5. They make our conditions more irrevocable. When a man comes to be ordinance-proof, prayer-proof, sermon and sacrament-proof, that none of these can enter a work on him, he is out-grown the power of ordinances, that man's condition is very near desperate.

There is nothing that makes the condition of the soul more desperate and unrecoverable than to the use of ordinances in a formal and unconscionable way, when a man hardens under means of softening. When a man's sore reopens under the bandage, no, when the bandage *increases* the sore, when that which should draw us near, sets us at further distance, this man's condition is *dangerous*. Scarcely one of many are worked on. When once a man can hear and pray and receive and yet retain his sin too *without disturbance*, and all this does not trouble him, no weapon will pierce him; no command, no threatening of the Word, no power of ordinances can move him. This man is a great danger to die in this condition. And the use of ordinances in a formal way brings men to such a condition. As the use of medicine in an ordinary way takes away its working; so the use of ordinances in a formal way takes off the edge and blunts the power of working on the spirit.

Well then, let me exhort you not only to be conscionable to use, but to a conscionableness in the use of this ordinance. And this lies in two things:

1. That you come with hearts habitually disposed. This lies also in two things:

1. To be brought out of a state of sin: 1. the power, 2. the practice, and 3. the love of all sin. For sin sets a distance between you and God in ordinances, it pollutes an ordinance; it indisposes you for acceptance in it.

2. To be brought into a state of grace, to have your nature changed, not partially, but universally and spiritually, not only to have new practices, but new principles. "Old things pass away, and all things become new."

2. This conscionableness in the use of ordinances, it lies in this that you come with hearts actually disposed, and that consists in two things: 1. examination. 2. excitation.

But of these I shall have occasion to speak larger in the following discourse.

Meeting God

There is yet another branch of the exhortation.

If it is that whoever has anything to do with any ordinance of God, and they meet God in it, O! then whenever you go to have something to do with any ordinance, be sure you take *Christ* with you. There is a necessity of this: 1. In regard of admission. 2. In regard of assistance. 3. In regard of acceptance.

1. In regard of admission, God is a consuming fire, and we are but dried stubble. There is no approaching of him but in Christ, in whom we have access with boldness to the throne of grace; God will not look pleasingly on you, if you come without Christ, there is no throng of grace without him; without Christ it is rather a bar or tribunal of *justice*, than a *throne of grace*. It is Christ who makes that which was a *Bar of Justice*, a *Bench of Mercy* (Eph. 1:2; Heb. 14:14-16; Heb. 10:12-13). In him we have admission. You go on this ordinance now, but do not go in the strength of your preparations but in the strength of Christ. Say, *Lord, I come alone in the merits of Christ, to partake of the merits of the Lord Jesus. I come in the blood of Christ, to partake of the blood of the Lord Jesus. I have endeavored to prepare to prepare and fit myself through your grace, but I do not look for admission through my preparations, but through the blood and mediation of Christ.*

2. There is a necessity of Christ in regard of assistance. You go on ordinances, but you have no strength to do them without Christ, for who is sufficient for these things? You might as well be set to move mountains, as to undertake

37

ordinances, without the strength of Christ, "Without me you can do nothing," Christ says (John 15). Without union with him, without communion with him, from him we must have both operating and co-operating strength, both inherent and assistant strength. Otherwise though you have grace, yet you will not be able to perform any work, nor exercise your own graces. It is he that must work all our works in us and for us; the inherent work of grace within us, and the required works of duty for us.[4] And blessed be that God, who has given to us what he requires of us, and has not only made precepts promises, but made promises performances.

3. There is a necessity of Christ in regard of acceptance. Our works, they are not only impotent, but impure too, as they come from us.[5] It is Christ that must put validity to them, and Christ that must put his own odors to them, Christ must put both his Spirit and merit to them, his grace to work them, and his blood to own them; whatever comes from his Spirit, is presented through his merit.[6]

---

[4] *Quod d re requirla ipse donasti prius.* Chrysostom.

[5] *Nihil ab homiue exit quan vis perfecto quod non sit aliqua macula inquinatum.* Calvin.

[6] *Merisu me um miseratio Domini, non sum pland meritis inove quandiu non fuerit ille inops miserationum. Dominue meminero justifie sua solius, ipsa enim est etc inea, etc.* Calvin *Instit.* Lib. 3. c. 17, Sect. 3, God does not look on the works of saints, *in foro stricti judis,* but *in foro Evangelis. cf.* Eph. 1:6.

And here is a great comfort; you look over your performances, and cannot see, however God can accept them. So much deadness, so little life, so much coldness; but God looks on them, not as yours, but as Christ's in whom not only our persons but our performances are accepted. Christ gives us his Spirit, and Christ is willing to own what we present by his Spirit, and God is willing to own, whatever is presented to him by his Son.

THE SECOND DOCTRINE

Well then, you have something to do with the ordinances of God, by these you draw near to God; but would you be admitted into the presence of God? Would you have God to hold out a golden scepter to you? Would you have grace and assistance to perform the work? Would you have acceptance when the work is done? O! get Christ to go along with you! And so much for the first doctrine, which is an introduction to the second.

That they who draw near to God in any ordinance must sanctify God in it.

In prosecution of which we shall do three things, we will *show:*

1. What it is to sanctify God in an ordinance.

2. How we must sanctify God in an ordinance.

3. Why we must sanctify God in an ordinance. And so we will also cover the application.

1. What does it mean to sanctify God in an ordinance?

To the sanctifying of God in an ordinance there is something required: 1. in the work, and, 2. in the workman.

1. *The work*, and that is, that it is an ordinance, such a one as he has instituted and set up, otherwise we cannot sanctify God in it, no more than the Papists in their blind devotions and superstitions. These offer strange fire. As God's benediction does not accompany anything further than it is an ordinance of his, so our sanctification of God extends no further than to his own ordinances, which he himself has set up and ordained; in other things we do not sanctify him, we dishonor him.

3. Something required in the workman. To say nothing here of the main requisite, which is, that he is in Christ. So for that we take for granted; and to qualify such a one to his ordinance. And in such a one there is something required in his head, and something in his heart.

1. In his head, and that is, first, that he conceives God correctly in his person and attributes. Secondly, and that he conceives aright of the ordinance itself. 1. That he conceives aright of God, that he has a right knowledge of God, right

conceptions of God in his nature, in his person, in his attributes, and of his Son. 2. Of his ordinances. 1. In the nature of them. 2. The use of them. 3. The fruit and benefit of them.

2. Something in his heart; and *that,*

First, that he brings holy affections to it; every ordinance of God requires the affections to be employed about it, and not only affections, but holy affections, such affections as do arise from a holy heart, and in this there is the spring. Unfound professors may sometime have some flashing in their devotions, as you see Herod, who heard John Baptist joyfully; they may have some affections but, 1. They are not holy affections. 2. Not such as arise from a principle, a spring within, because there's no root. 3. They are not orderly affections, but land-floods for a time. 4. They are not transforming affections, such as change the heart; and therefore such affections may be exercised, yet they leave a man as they found him, and such a man cannot sanctify God in an ordinance.

Secondly, there must not only be holy affections, but such as are suitable to the ordinance and work in hand. It is possible to have holy affections, them stirred up in an ordinance, and yet not sanctify God in it, because these are not suitable to the ordinance, *Nihil ad em,* nothing to the work in hand, they are not suitable with the present ordinance that God has called the soul out on, as I could show you at large.

Thirdly, there must not only be holy affections, and suitable affections, but those excited and stirred up. A man may have holy, and such as are suitable to an ordinance, as the saints have in the frame of grace, and yet not sanctify God in an ordinance, because they are not excited and stirred up. "Stir up the gift of God in thee," says the Apostle to Timothy, that is, excite and blow up the gifts of grace of God in you, ἀναζωπυρεῖν τὸ χάρισμα τοῦ θεου (2 Tim. 1:6).

When you are to draw near with God, you must stir up those affections, and graces which are within you. And this requires a matter of pains; affections are not ever at hand, nor ever at command. A man does not have his heart under lock and key. And therefore God in mercy considering and respecting our weakness, has graciously allotted a time of preparation before he calls us forth on the performance of an ordinance, that so we might get our affections up, our hearts in tune. Once indeed we read that men were called out on an ordinance, and were strained with time to prepare themselves according to the preparation of the sanctuary, as in Hezekiah's time. They had habitual preparation, but lacked actual. In that case, the lack of time, God pardoned it, but it was prayed for, it was fought for, and fought for earnestly (2

Chron. 39:18-19). But we read another time, that God punished the lack of this actual preparation, and stirring up their graces and affections; yes, and punished severely, with the weakness, sickness, death of many of the Corinthians, "For this cause many are sick, many are weak, many are fallen asleep," yet were they habitually prepared (1 Cor. 11:1). They died for a proper use of the ordinance by God's judgment on them. And this in the New Testament? Certainly so.

God takes it for a great dishonor to him, that we should come slightly on so great a work, to which all the affections we have, and all the affections we can stir up, are little enough. We had need call in for all the strength of grace; no, all the succors in Christ, and all the supplies and aids of the Spirit, to the performance of it. By this you may gather, what it is to sanctify God in an ordinance.

2. How must we sanctify God in an ordinance?

To sanctify God in an ordinance, there is required something: 1. antecedent. 2. concomitant. And, 3. subsequent.

1. Something antecedent, or before. 2. Something in the time. 3. Afterwards. These are generals, which belong to every particular ordinance, as I could show you at large.

When you come to hear the Word, there is something required of you. As, 1. Meditation; into what place, into whose presence, about what business we go. 2. Examination, of 1.

43

Our sins, that here we might have them slain by the sword of the Spirit, in the Ministry of the Word. 2. Our graces, that here we might have them strengthened and nourished by the spiritual food of our souls. 3. Prayer for the minister, for the congregation, ourselves, that a blessing may be on.

2. In the time is required, 1. reverence, 2. attention, 3. submission of spirit and humility, as well as 4. faith.

3. Afterward, prayer again, which must be the *Alpha and Omega*. 2. Meditation. And, 3. fruitfulness and obedience.

So for the prayer, there is required, 1. Before meditation, preparation. 3. In the time, faith, service, humility, suitableness of spirit, and enlarged desires. 3. Afterward such a deportment and demeanor as is suitable to such who call on God, as to depart from sin, to apply our heart to obedience, to expect the answer and return of our prayers (Psalm 5:3). "In the morning I will direct my prayer (וָאֲצַפֶּה) and look up." There are two military words used here. He would not only pray, but *marshal up* his prayers, put them in array; and when he had done, he would be as a spy on a tower to see whether he prevailed, whether he got the day.

But to pass these, and come to the ordinance we are to enter on the sacrament. To sanctify God, in which, there is required, 1. something before, 2. something in the time, and 3. something after.

1. Something before, which may be laid down in these two heads.

1. Habitual. 2. Actual.

1. Habitual preparation, which consists in the whole frame of grace and sanctification. It is an ordinance only for such who are sanctified. We are to have, 1. A saving knowledge of God, of ourselves. 2. Lively faith. 3. A true repentance, 4. Love. 5. Hunger and thirst after Christ. This is a feast, and there is no coming without a stomach. 6. Thankfulness.

2. Actual preparation, and that consists in the actual stirring up, and exciting of those graces which are in you. There must be a new exciting faith, a new exercise of repentance, the latitude and extent of it, for all sin; but especially for those sins which you have committed since the last time you renewed your Covenant with God, in this ordinance. So a stirring up of our love, affections, our desires, hunger and thirst. This he required before, which because it is so largely treated on by many learned and godly Divines, I shall purposefully wave any further treaty of it, referring you in this point, to what they have so largely written (Mr. Dike on the *Sacrament*, and Mr. Downame).

Passing this therefore, we fall on the second, which has not been so frequently taught.

2. As there is something then required before, viz. Habitual and actual *preparation*. So secondly, there is something required in the time; and that is the exercises of graces, and gracious dispositions. A man may be a sanctified person, and yet not sanctify God in this ordinance, if he does not exercise those graces, and gracious dispositions which God requires here, and are suitable to the quality and nature of the ordinance.

1. Now the first and great grace that here is to be exercised is Faith. Faith is the great grace which gives admission unto this ordinance, and faith is the great grace that is to be exercised, and to run through the use of it.

FAITH

Concerning which we shall desire to unfold three *things:*

1. What act of faith is here to be exercised.

2. On what object we must exercise our faith here.

3. For what benefits faith must here be exercised.

For the first, viz. what act of faith is here to be exercised. There are these two main acts of faith. 1. An act of recumbence. 2. An act of apprehension and application of

Christ. Both these may be exercised here, and to our spiritual benefit.[7]

By the one we go over to Christ, by the other we bring Christ over to us.

The first act of faith gives us an interest in all the benefits of Christ, though as yet the soul is not able to bring home to itself the great revenue of mercy and grace, which Christ has purchased, and the soul has an interest in. The second act of faith brings it all home. In the former, God makes Christ ours, and we his; in the latter we make him ours. This is Christ in his blood and merits, Christ in his grace and Spirit, Christ in all his dongs and sufferings; so far as he is communicable to poor sinners. Now there is not much difference between these two acts. The difference is not in the nature and essence of the grace, both are faith, and saving faith; nor in the fruits and benefits, both give a man union and communion with Christ, *etc.* But the difference is in the measures, and degrees, in the comforts of it. To the first there goes a conviction of sin, a manifestation and clearing of the promise, a persuasion of the truth, fullness, freeness, suitableness, and goodness of the promise. And on all this here is a rolling, a resting on Christ. And the later, is but a further

---

[7] *Fided potest babere aliquem modum dubitationis, salud fide.* Davenant. *Fidei certisudo importer firmitatem abdeaesionis, non quietatioinem intellectum.* Aquinas.

degree, a bringing over a home all this to its own self. In the former act, a soul has communion with all the benefits of Christ. It's such an act of faith, as gives a soul union with the person and that cannot be without communion with the privileges and benefits. In this later, there is but a clearer apprehension of it. In the first, we go over to Christ. In the later, we are apprehended of Christ; in the later we apprehend Christ (Phil. 3:11).

Now, to the answer, what act of faith is here to be exercised. To this I say, that that act of faith, which apprehends and applies Christ, is most suitable to this ordinance of the sacrament; here is this called a taking of Christ, a receiving of Christ, a feeding on Christ, eating his flesh; and drinking his blood; all which show this act is most suitable to the ordinance.

Here we have an offer of Christ, and this act is most suitable to take him as offered. And the more strength we have to apply and bring Christ home, the more we feed on him, the more we are nourished, and built up.

But though this act of faith is more suitable to the ordinance, yet we shut not out the other from the comfort and benefit of it. That which gives the soul union with Christ, does give it communion with all the benefits of Christ. Christ and his benefits go together. Yet I could wish that everyone who has done this first act of faith, would work it up one degree higher, to apprehend and apply Christ in the promises of grace, seeing according to the measure of your faith, and feeding on Christ; such is the measures of the benefit by Christ here. But however, be not discouraged, such as are weak in faith, will Christ receive. If he has a care, others shall not reject them for the weakness, but bid them to receive them, much more will he himself receive them; and whom he will receive, shall receive him.

If therefore you are weak in applying faith, and you cannot bring Christ over to you, go you over to Christ; if you cannot fully apprehend him, let him apprehend you, cast yourself into his arms; by this act, set your seal to God's truth and expect here in this ordinance that God should put his seal to your heart, by assuring (Phil. 3:12).[8] So much for the first, what act of faith is here to be exercised. We come to the second.

2. On what object must the act of faith be terminated here? You must know there are many objects of faith in general; as God himself in the unity of essence, and trinity of persons, the Word of God, the promises of God. But there is but one object of justifying faith, and that is Christ, God-man,

---

[8] *In langaida fide magis nos apprehendi mur a Christo, quaim quod nos ipsu n apprehensamus.* Chen.

49

the Mediator, "To him give all the Prophets witness; that whoever believes in him shall receive remission of sins," (Acts 10:13; Gen. 3:15). This is the object on which the faith of Adam was terminated, the seed of the woman, and by it was justified, and had his recovery after the fall (Gen. 3:15).This is that object on which the faith of Abraham, who was the father of the faithful, was terminated, who saw his day, and rejoiced; it was not the believing of the *promise* of the seed, but in the *promised seed*. To him also did the eyes of the faithful look under the Law, through the shadows and sacrifices, and were justified by Christ to be, as we are now by Christ exhibited.

And on him must our faith be terminated, not only in the first act of faith for justification, but also in the exercise of it in this ordinance, for the further assurance of justification, and increase of sanctification.

And do not let it seem strange to you, we are not so much to deal with a promise here, as with the thing promised; nor to feed on a promise, as on Christ himself by faith, to eat his flesh, and drink his blood, "This is my body, *etc.*" (Matt. 25:16, *Corpus Christi est pahalum fidei*). Christ is the meat for the hand of faith to receive, the mouth of faith to eat, as he says, "My flesh is meat indeed, and my blood is drink indeed" (John 6:25). You may make use of the promises here; the sacrament is the seal to every promise in the covenant. But the matter of the sacrament indeed, and that on which we are chiefly to feed, is Christ himself. Christ as he is laid out to us in his death and sufferings, on which feeding, we get spiritual nourishment for grace, and death of sin. The blood of Christ, like the waters appointed for the trial of jealousy, has a double property, to kill, and to make fruitful; to kill our sins, and make our graces grow; to rot our sins, and ripen our grace.

Well then, remember that great dish you feed on as this feast is Christ himself.[9] You cannot feed on Christ; he does not only give us title and interests in them, but appetite to them. If you feed on him, your stomach will be quicker to feed on them; no, if you feed on him, you feed on all the promises, and have an interest in all the good of them, the sweet of all the promises is tasted in Christ. All the promises are folded up in Christ, and you cannot feed on him, but you feed on all, and have the blessing of every one in particular. The promises of justification, sanctification, subduing of corruptions, increase of grace, upholding in grace, interest in glory, they are all of them folded up in Christ, he is all.

The promise does not justify, but Christ does justify, Christ does sanctify; you get nothing from the promise separate from Christ, but all the good of the promise comes in

---

[9] *Christo sublato nebilrest at in sacramentis, preter inave spectaculum Div. in Col Christus est substantia sacramentorum; ect. Ejus opera tio est ipsa vita sacramentorum.*

by Christ, and therefore here terminate your faith. And so much for the second, on what object we must terminate our faith. We come to the third.

For what benefit must faith here be exercised?

First, faith must not be here acted for your justification; it is required you should be justified persons, have your sins forgiven before you come close. He that comes close under the guilt of sin goes away with more guilt, and his former guilt is doubled and confirmed on him. So that for this benefit, faith is not to be acted, as we shall show hereafter.

Secondly, faith must not be here acted for regeneration; it is required a man should be born again, be in the state of grace, sanctified, *before* he comes close. Here is the multiplying of grace, but no begetting of grace. As in the miracle of loaves, there was no new bread created, but a multiplying of the bread they had (Matt. 14:19). So here is no giving of grace where there is none, but a multiplying of grace where it is. Where grace is, there it is increased, but it is not here begotten. A man may come to the Word, though he is graceless, because the Word is an ordinance set up for the gathering of men, and begetting souls to Christ (Rom. 10:14). But none are to come to the sacrament, but such as are begotten anew; the sacrament is not the font, it is not the place where men are born, but the table where men are nourished; it is not the seed of the new birth, but the meat of the new born, we must be born before we eat, bred before fed, begotten before nourished. If we come close without grace, we shall go away graceless and worse than we came in particular then.

Faith must here be exercised for the further assurance of our justification. God has cast down the soul by the minister of the Word, he has discovered and revealed the promise, brought the soul over to the promise, up which it rests, and is justified, and hither we come to be further assured of it.[10] This was one end why the Sacrament was set up. We know the strongest are but weak in faith; there is no such assurance in the world, as to expel all doubts and fears, though to overcome them, but though they be suspended in their acting's for a time, and well subdued and conquered, yet they are not altogether expelled. If they were, then were there no need of the Sacrament for this end, to confirm and strengthen faith, and so one of the ends wherefore God set up this ordinance were in vain to that man. But I say there is no man so sure, but may be surer. There are degrees of assurance as well as faith, and so may we grow up in assurance as well as faith. And now for the further assurance of our justification,

---

[10] *Fides non totis ses vincit ornem dubitationem.* Davenant. *Fides potest babese aliquem modum dubitationis,* Calvin. Fid.

God to the covenant of grace and mercy, in which he promised the free pardon of sin, has annexed the seal of the covenant, by which we may be more assured.

Indeed here is no need of this in respect of God, our justification is sure with him, his intention is as good as his promise, his promise as his oath, his oath as his seal. But it was God's goodness to us, pitying the weakness of our faith; he stooped below himself, and was not only content to give us his promise, but to confirm it with his oath, the great seal of heaven, and to all this to afford his sacraments, to seal up all unto us that we might have strong assurance and consolation (Heb. 6:18). It was to this end, to assure us, who have such unbelieving hearts, that God gave word on word, promise on promise, oath to oath, seal to seal, heaping mountain on mountain, and all to confirm our staggering hearts (Heb. 18:19). That we might be strong in him, when weak in ourselves, faithful in him, when fearful in ourselves, steadfast in him, when we stagger in ourselves.

And how should we exercise faith here, and go doubting away? How shall we go away trembling after all this confirmation? An oath among men is the end of all controversy, the concluding of all difference and disputes, and shall not God's oath prevail so much with you? Why do you suffer return of fears and doubts after such a seal?[11] Woe be to us, if we will not believe God, no not on his oath. Do you desire better security? You shall never have it, you cannot. If you would come up to God, and take his security, how could you doubt?

2. A second benefit for the compassing of which faith must be exercised, *etc.* is the increase of our graces, or perfecting of our sanctification. My brethren, we are weak in grace, you know how much infidelity, and how little faith, how much enmity, how little love, how much obstinacy, how little pliable conformity to his will, what a deal of formality, how little power, what hardness of heart, how little brokenness of spirit for sin, *etc.*? And being weak in grace, there is necessity that these graces should be nourished. As there is necessity of daily bread, for the nourishing and upholding of our bodies; so there is necessity of spiritual food for the nourishing of grace in our souls. And as there is necessity of our nourishment, so is there necessity our nourishment should come from Christ, he is the start of nourishment. As in natural life the same way we are begotten, the same way we are nourished. So in spiritual life, Christ he is the breeder, and so he is the feeder of grace in us; he is the

---

begetter and he is the nourisher.[12] From Christ we have our graces, he is the fountain from whose fullness we receive grace for grace in our regeneration, and he is the nourishment of whose fullness we receive grace to grace in our sanctification.[13] Hence he is called the "Bread of Life," not only because he begets life in dead men, but because he nourishes and maintains life in living men. He is *panis spiritualis*, spiritual bread, in the word to beget life; and *panis Sacramentalis*, bread in the sacrament, or sacramental bread, to nourish and to maintain life begotten; and hereafter he shall be *panis aeternalis*, our daily bread in heaven, to preserve us in holiness with happiness to all eternity. And as there is a necessity of nourishment, and nourishment by Christ, so Christ for this end, that we might be nourished, has set up this ordinance of the Sacrament, for the nourishment of the saints in grace, for the strengthening our faith, to which it has a proper influence, being the seal of the covenant, and for the increasing our sorrow and repentance, to which it has the like influence, being the representation of Christ wounded, broken, bleeding for sin; who looks on Christ bleeding, but his heart must bleed, *etc.*? And so of the rest.

---

[12] *Do moto quo penramu, nutrimur.*
[13] *Gratiam gritie ascumulatam.*

Christ is a full fountain, and unwilling to be a sealed fountain to you; he is a treasury of grace, and unwilling to be locked up, and therefore has been so gracious, as to set up an ordinance, not only to be a seal, but an instrument or conduit pipe to convey grace for us from him the fountain of all grace; which nourishment he does convey unto us by virtue of our union and communion with him and application of him to us in these ordinances; which though they are all secret ways of conveyance of nourishment, and underground, that the world cannot see, yet there is real nourishment brought down to the soul, by which the soul goes home in a better frame, faith more increased, affections more enlarged, our love more enflamed, our desires more quickened, and yet more satisfied.[14]

Question. But I know you will ask of me, how faith is exercised here, for the drawing down of life and nourishment from Christ in this ordinance?

Answer. For the answer of which in *brief*:

1. Faith looks on Christ as the treasury and common stock of grace, in whom dwells all fullness, all our fullness; faith looks on him as the universal principle of life and root of holiness. God did not give him the Spirit in measure (John 1:14, 18; 3:14; Col. 1:19; 3:3, 9).

---

[14] *Gratia de rivitur a Christo, 1 Efficacia operatiotiv 2. Beneficio intercession 3. Merito passionis 4. Virtute applicationnis.*

2. Faith casts its eye on the promise for the conveyance of grace from him; it sees a promise for derivation of grace from him to us. Faith works, *virtute promissi*, by virtue of the promise.[15] Where there is no promise, there can be no faith, and therefore faith discovers that there may be communion and participation with this fullness; there are such promises made, "that of his fullness we shall receive grace for grace" (John 1:16) and Christ is "made unto us wisdom, righteousness, sanctification," (1 Cor. 1:30) and he came that we might have life, and have it in abundance (John 10:10).

3. Faith looks on this ordinance as an instrument, a means which God has set up for the conveying of life and nourishment from Christ. Though God can do it without, yet in God's ordinary way, ordinances are the means of conveying of life from him to us.

4. Now then, faith being steeled by such considerations as these, that there is a fullness in Christ, that there is a promise of this fullness to be made over to us, and that the Sacrament is an ordinance by which God, as by an instrument, will convey of this fullness of Christ to a poor soul. Faith goes over to Christ, and by virtue of the promise, applying and feeding on Christ, draws down further life and nourishment from him to the soul. As one said of the tree of

---

[15] *Ille est canalis gratiae; etc. ab illa nolis omnes revul dark vantur.* Davenant.

Christ's ascension, though the fruit were high, and above our reach, yet if we touch him by the hand of faith, and tongue of prayer, all will fall down on us. So here, if we can but touch him with the hand of faith, though a palsy hand, though a weak and trembling hand; if we can but go to him with a praying heart, Christ can withhold nothing from us.

And after this manner does faith form a prayer to him, "Lord, you know I am weak in grace, you see my faith is feeble, my love cold, my desires faint, my obedience small; but you have all fullness of grace, you are the Fountain, and this Fountain is opened here, you are the Treasury, and this Treasury is here unlocked. Those grace I have, though weak, you beget them and will not you now nourish them? From you I had the being of grace, and from you I must have the nourishing. You have set up this ordinance as a means to convey grace, and you have promised to remember them that are in your way (Isa. 64:5), therefore help," *etc.* Besides, may faith say, "Lord, you have been pleased to implant me into Christ, and shall I die for lack of nourishment? You have made me a member of Christ, and shall I decay and wither for lack of influence?" O! Never let it be said, that a branch of Christ shall wither and decay for want of nourishment, when there is so much in the root; let it never be said, that a member of Christ should wither and die for want of influence and life, seeing there is so much in the head. "You came that I might have life, yes, and have it in abundance (1 John 10:10). Why, Lord, my graces are weak, here are dying affections, dying dispositions, dying graces, O! Come down before I die, strengthen the things that are ready to die in me. You have raised me from the death of sin, let me not again drop into the same grave (Rev. 3:2); you have worked graces in me, let them not decay for lack of life when such abundance in you."

In this way Christ forms in the heart a crying out for Christ nourishing the believer in the sacrament. The work of grace is called a *forming of Christ in the soul*, and Christ nourishes and feeds himself, his own graces here (Gal. 4:9). Christ in the sacrament nourishes Christ begotten in the heart by the Word. And the soul feeding on Christ by faith is further changed into his image. In our corporal feeding, the meat is changed into the nature of the eater, but in our spiritual feeding, the eater is changed to the nature of the meat eaten, the believer into the nature of Christ, "While beholding him as in a glass, we are also changed into his image," (1 Cor. 3:18). So does faith feed on Christ, and draw down nourishment for the strength of every grace in us, *etc.* And according to the measure of faiths feeding, such is the proportions and measure of nourishment conveyed. As the stomach sends down nourishment to all parts, from the supply of blood, which it has fed on; or, as the liver having drawn down and made blood from the nourishment in the stomach, diffuses and spreads abroad, and sends to every part some. So faith having fed on Christ here sends down nourishment to all the graces. Or, as in a feast, you send portions to your poor brethren; so faith having feasted itself on Christ sends down portions to her sister graces. All our graces have a dependence on faith, and faith on Christ; our graces depend on faith as a Mediator to our Mediator. As that grace which has immediately to do with Christ, from where it fetches supply and provision for all the rest. That is the second benefit faith is here to be acted for.

3. The third benefit that faith is here to be exercised on Christ for is the further subduing and conquering of our corruptions. Faith has a double work to do; it works in heaven, and it works in earth. As it works in heaven for the justification of sin, so it works in earth for the mortification of sin; and here in this ordinance is faith acted on Christ for the further killing of sin. Faith has a special art in going over to Christ, and fetching from him such help as is suitable to the necessities of the soul. If we are weak in graces, faith can go over to Christ for the strengthening of them. If corruption be strong, faith can go over to Christ for the subduing and conquering of them. And by making use of the merit, power, promise, Spirit of Christ, gets strength from him for the

subduing of unruly lusts, untamed corruptions. "Why," will faith say, "Lord, you have promised to subdue all to yourself, O! Therefore set your power against the power of my lusts. These sons of Zerviah are too strong for me, but not for you. I am burdened with a dead heart, a hard heart, unbelieving heart, *etc.* But never was there heart so hard, but you cannot break it, never heart so dead but you cannot quicken it. There is life enough in you for all the sons and daughters of death in the world. O! That therefore you would quicken me, that you would break me." So faith makes us of Christ here for the subduing of corruptions.

And let me tell you, there is a special art, dexterity and skill which faith has, by which it forms such conceptions of Christ, as are ever suitable to the present necessity of the soul, by which it gets more speedy relief.

1. If there is a return of guilt on the soul, and burden on the conscience, faith looks on Christ in blood, Christ a Priest, a *sacrifice* for sin.

2. If the soul labors under ignorance, faith looks on him as the great Prophet of the Church, and says, *Lord you have taken on you to be the great Prophet of the Church, you have promised we shall be all taught of God* (John 6:45; Isa. 14:13; Jer. 31:34). *O! Therefore teach me, instruct me, etc.* It is not so suitable to look on

Christ as a Priest, when we desire he should do the work of Prophet.

3. If we are weak in grace, faith looks on him as the universal fountain and principle of grace, one who has all fullness in him, able to fill a world of hearts with grace, though they were never so barren or empty; and so goes over to him for strength, *etc.*

4. If we labor under the pollution of sin, faith looks on Christ as a refiner, a purifier, a purger of his people from sin (Malachi 3:2). He is as one who did not come only to be a Redeemer, but a *refiner*; not only a Savior, but a *sanctifier* of his people (Eph. 5:6; Titus 2:14).

5. And so, if corruptions are strong, faith looks on him as a King, who is able to subdue and conquer unruly affections, and to bring everything into subjection to himself.

God has not only furnished Christ with fullness of supply to answer every need of the soul, but God has given to Christ diversity of titles, that we might conceive of him not only as a full, but as a suitable good to every necessity of the soul. And God, having so diversely represented Christ to our understandings, as a Prophet, a Priest, a King, a Refiner, *etc.* faith forms such conceptions of Christ, as are most suitable to the present necessity of the soul.

4. A fourth benefit for which faith may be exercised in this ordinance is for deliverance out of temptations, (1 Cor. 10:13; 2 Cor. 12:9.[16] You have been long assaulted by Satan; you have felt the blows and buffets of Satan many years; God has not only promised to support you and succor you in this condition, but God has promised to deliver you out of this condition, "The God of peace shall tread down Satan under your feet shortly," (Rom. 16:20). Why, now exercise faith to search out these promises God has made; go over to Christ, not only for strength and support in the condition, but for victory and deliverance out of it. These days, there are not only God's sealing, but God's *performing* days. God does not only here put his seal to every promise folded up in the Covenant, but he is ready here to make performance of the things he has promised. And therefore go gather a catalogue of promises, which suites with you condition, spread them before God, and here search them out in this ordinance.

So you see the first grace which is to be exercised in this ordinance, namely faith. And I have showed you, 1. What action, 2. on what object, and, 3. for what benefits faith is here to be exercised. I have named four, but here is not all; the sacrament is the seal of the whole Covenant, and whatever particular benefits are folded up in the great draught and

---

[16] *Una sitius sine peccato, nullus sine tentatione.*

Covenant of God, here you may exercise faith for compassing and obtaining them. Wherever there is a promise in the Word, there is work for faith to sue it out in this ordinance, which is the seal to all, *etc.*

By the way then, this may discover to us, where the fault is, when we return home, our faith never the more strengthened, our hearts never the more warmed, our graces never the more nourished, our corruptions never the more weakened. It is a shrewd sign faith did not play its part in the mount. It is great suspicion that your faith did *succumbere in conatu, did fail and sink in the encounter.* Faith was entrusted in this employment to go over to Christ for these benefits, and your faith did fail in the undertaking, therefore God suspends the bestowing of these benefits, because you suspend your faith.

A man may halt after his striving with God, and yet overcome, as Jacob did; but when a man's spirit halts in striving with God, when we do not strive fully with God, there is little hope of prevailing. Well then, if you see not the fruit and benefit you expected to come into your soul in the use of this ordinance, charge your faith with it, and bewail the weakness of it. And for the future put it to its burden, let it have its full and perfect work, and you will then find the comfort and fruit of it. Never did faith touch Christ in any ordinance, but virtue came from him. But so much for the first grace.

REPENTANCE

2. A second grace which is here to be exercised in the use of this ordinance, and requisite to the sanctification of God in it, is *repentance*.

The sacraments are the crucifixes of Christ, in which Christ is represented as crucified afresh before our eyes. The bread broken preaches to us the breaking of Christ. The wine poured forth does preach to us the blood of Christ poured forth for our sins. And who is it that can with the eye of faith; look on a broken Christ, but with a broken heart? A wounded Christ, but with a wounded spirit? A bleeding Christ, but with a bleeding soul? God has made in nature the same organ for the seeing and weeping. And in grace he who sees clearly, weeps thoroughly, "The eye will affect the heart" (Lam. 3:5).

The Passover under the Law was to be eaten with *bitter* herbs. So Christ the true Passover is here to be eaten with *bitterness* of soul. As it was prophesied, "They shall look on him whom they have pierced, and shall lament and mourn, first seeing, and then weeping," (Zech. 12:10). We see this in two *ways:*

1. Historical; 2. Spiritual.

1. Historical mourning; there is a natural tenderness in men and women, by which their hearts yearn and melt to hear the relation, or behold the fight of some sad story. Such a one as Augustine confesses he had when he read the sad story of Dido. And yet his heart was hard, he could not mourn for sin. Or such a one as they had, whom Christ blamed in the Gospel, who lamented the cruel usage of Christ out of natural compassion only, to whom he says, "O daughters of Jerusalem, weep not for me." Of this the early church father speaks, "It is not necessary you lament his passion, so much as your sins, which have caused his passion."[17] There is a kind of natural tenderness in men and women, which yet is often joined with hardness of heart for sin. As a historical faith, with spiritual unbelief, and a historical love, with spiritual enmity; so a natural tenderness, with spiritual hardness of heart for sin.

2. There is a spiritual mourning, which arises from spiritual grounds and causes, and tends to spiritual ends. A sorrow which is caused by faith, looking on heart-melting promises, or taking up heart breaking considerations, or beholding a heart-softening object, by which faith draws waters out of the fountains of the soul for sin, as you have it in

---

[17] *Homi ni nou est necessarium ut Christ ii in ipsius passion deploret, sed magu ut sepsum in Christo.*

1 Samuel 7:6 they drew water (as out of a well) and poured it forth before the Lord. And this is that sorrow which is here to be exercised, which will melt and mellow the heart, and cause it to be more mellow the heart, and cause it to be more fruitful in obedience. Never does the garden of graces better grow, then after such a shower of repentant tears. And therefore God preserves these springs in the soul, to water the seeds of grace, and make us more fruitful, which it surely does when they are sun-shine flowers, such showers in which the sun appears, Christ is not hid from the eye of faith.

And, my brethren, here are many things in this ordinance, which if but looked on with the eye of faith, will open all the springs of sorrow in the soul, and call forth all the water in him. Bellarmine he lays down twelve considerations to provoke sorrow, as the miseries of mankind by nature, the sad condition of the souls in Purgatory, and such like stuff. But we need not be beholding to him for such considerations as these to occasion mourning. Here is enough in the Sacrament presented to the eye of faith, to open all the springs you have, and if you had a fountain of tears to spend them all for sin. We will name some particulars here which draw our mourning's.

1. Here is a discovery of the love and sweetness of God, in giving his Son to die for us. "For God so loved the world"

(John 3:16), *etc.* enough to cause us to mourn that ever we offended. "O that God should be more tender to us than to his own Son, not spare his Son that he might spare us, give him to die, that we might live, pour the curse on him, that the blessing might be poured on us!" O how should this affect us! Who can think of this and withhold from tears?[18]

2. Here is presented to us the sufferings and breakings of Christ, enough to break our hardest hearts. 1. The sufferings of Christ, *in se*, in themselves, as those on his body; what breakings, what woundings, what scourgings, what crownings, piercings, did he endure in his body and those in his soul? What conflicts and strugglings did he undergo with the wrath of God, the terrors of death, the powers of darkness? O! what weight, what burden, and what wrath did he undergo when his soul was heavy *unto death*? Beset with terrors, as the word signifies, when he drank that bitter cup, that cup mingled with curses, which if man or angel had but sipped of, it would have sunk them into hell; no, it made him, who was God as well as man, sanctified by the Spirit, supported with the Deity, comforted by Angels, sweat such sweat as never man sweat; drops, clods of blood, as the word implies (θρόμβοι αἵματος (Luke 22:44)).

---

[18] *Quis temperet a laobrymis.*

2. Consider them *in causa*, as the *meriting cause* of all our good, the procurers of all our peace, salvation, *etc.*

He was wounded, that we might be healed, scourged, that we might be solaced, drunk the cup of wrath, a bitter cup, to procure all our sweet draughts. He was slain, says Isaiah, but not for himself, "He was wounded for our transgressions, broken for our iniquities, the chastisement of our peace was on him, and by his stripes are we healed" (Isa. 53:5-8).

3. Consider them as *effectus peccati*, as the *effects* of our sin, as those things our sins brought on him, and needs must this melt and thaw our icy and stony hearts. O! will the soul say, "It has been I who have been the traitor, the murderer, (*sulvere gelicidium*) my sins which have been bloody instruments to slay the Lord of Glory. I have sinned, you suffered, it was I that did eat the sour grapes, yet your teeth were set on edge; I have been your death, yet your death has given me life; I have wounded you, yet you have healed me; yea, and even out of that wound my sins made you send a covering to heal me" (Ezek. 18). This consideration must need fill the heart with sorrow, "They shall look on him whom they have pierced," and how shall this sight affect them, why it follows, "They shall mourn and be in bitterness of soul, as one in bitterness for their first-born" (Zech. 12:10).

They say, if one man kills another, and you bring the murderer into the place, where the slain person lies, the dead will bleed afresh. We are the murderers of Christ, and we come here to an ordinance where Christ is represented in his blood as broken and wounded for our sins. O! that our hearts might bleed as he bleeds afresh to us, so that we might bleed afresh for him. A prince will weep himself when the pauper is whipped for him. But how should the pauper mourn when the prince is scourged *for him*? My brethren, there is infinite more disproportion between Christ and us, than between the prince and the pauper, the Lord and the slave. And how can we then look on him as wounded, scourged, and pierced for us, and not be affected with, afflicted for our sins, the cause of it. Bernard says, "If you would be conformable to Christ (in the Sacrament) as you behold a broken and a bleeding Christ; so labor to behold him with a broken bleeding heart," *Si vis ipsun cognoscere, sicut se fregit, it ate frasge.* Look on him in this ordinance, as Mary looked on him on the cross; when Simeon's prophecy was fulfilled, that a sword should pass through her soul (Luke 2:35), for then indeed did a sword pass through her soul, when she saw him pierced on the cross. So when you see him pierced and broken in the sacrament, which is the lively representation of Christ broken; O! that then is might be as a spear to our hearts! As a sword to our spirits, that we by our sins have wounded and pierced him!

A Humble and Holy Reverence

This is the second grace to be exercised in this ordinance. And beside these two there are many more to be exercised here, viz. Our love to God, our hungering and thirsting after Christ. There is that in Christ represented to the eye of faith in this Sacrament, that calls out for all the affections, dispositions, and desires in you; you cannot see Christ here, but it will make every grace within you stir, every disposition within you to move, every wheel go. Who can see him, but love him, who is so exceeding lovely? Who can see him, but prize him, who is so exceeding precious? Who can see him but desire him, who is so exceeding desirable? Who can see him but delight in him, who is the joy and delight of the soul? You cannot possibly see him here, but all the powers of the soul will be uplifted. Your judgments to prize him, your wills to choose him, and make a new match with him; your affection to love him embrace him; delight in him. And the clearer your fight is here of Christ by faith, the more will your hearts be stirred, your spirits moved. Men that sit here as logs and lumps of clay, never stirred, never taken up, they do not see Christ, they see no higher than the table, the Bread and Wine, and therefore dead and senseless. O! But if one crevice of your hearts opened, to let in but one beam, one glimpse of Christ, it would set you all on a burning heavenly fire, this would warm you indeed. But besides these graces to be exercised, there is required some demeanors in the soul, in this ordinance, if we would sanctify God in it.

1. A humble and holy reverence, which is the fruit of that dread and fear of God which is in the heart. There is abundance of lightness, looseness and vanity in the spirits of men by nature. And the Majesty and dread of that great God, with whom we have something to do in this ordinance, must consolidate and make our spirits weighty in these great ordinances. The sacrament of the Lord's Supper is called *Eucharist*, it is a gratulatory service, and God is fearful in praises (Exod. 15:11) which has special respect to the affection wherewith you are to praise him, εὐχαριστήσας (1 Cor. 11:24).

2. There is required a discharge and dismissing of all worldly thoughts and business. When Abraham went up to the mount to sacrifice, he left his servants in the valley. You are now to go up to the mount, where God appears. O! leave all your servile affections, your worldly thoughts in the valley. And if any enter, do as Abraham did by the birds that would have eaten up the sacrifice, chase them away; do by them as

73

you do by straggling beggars, give them their pass, and send them away.

In the temple, though there was so much flesh for sacrifice, yet there was not one fly appeared stirring; O! that it might be so with us this day! That not one thought might arise on our hearts, unsuitable to the place and work in hand. It is a thing unbefitting these great employments, to have our hearts and thoughts taken up with other business; what have you to do here with yours shops, your bags, your containers? What have you here to do with things of this world?

O! do not make this place an *exchange*, a shop for merchandise; men are not able to do business in neither a crowd, nor you so great a business as this, in a crowd of thoughts. But this is the misery, you are servants and slaves to the world at other times, and therefore the world will master you now. If you pass over your hearts to the service of the world at other times, the world will make you serve it now. Because you do not have spiritual hearts, in your temporal employments, therefore have you carnal hearts in your spiritual employments. The less of the Sabbath in the week, the more you shall find of the week in the Sabbath. The less spiritual you are in the affairs of the earth, the more carnal you will be in the employments of heaven. This is certain; if the world once took your heart it will take your mind also. I say, if ever the world leavens your hearts, it will also poison your minds; it is as leaven diffuses itself throughout the whole man. And therefore as Christ said of the leaven of the Pharisees, "Take heed of the leaven of the Pharisees," *i.e.* hypocrisy (for if once the heart is leavened with that it will sour the mind. If the principles are unfound, then are the purposes also, and performances too, *etc.*). So I say here, beware of the leaven of worldly-mindedness, if ever you would sanctify God in this ordinance. Beware of that, this will sour the soul and make all you do to be carnal and fleshly. I tell you, if you are servants of the world at other times, the world will command and master you now. So much shall serve for the second general head, *what is required in the time for the sanctification of this ordinance.* We come to the third.

LABOR TO SEE FRUIT

To the sanctifying God in an ordinance, is required something after.

That now which is required afterward is, that you labor to see the fruit of this ordinance to run down through your lives. You exercised faith, labor to see your heart more established in assurance of pardon. See your graces more strengthened, your corruptions more weakened. I will name only two things which are to follow the performance of this ordinance, if ever you would sanctify God in it.

1. Thankfulness
2. Obedience.

THANKFULNESS

1. Thankfulness: return home now, is your heart full of the benefits of the Lord; so your heart full of praises to the Lord. Angel's employments are most suitable to angel's food; you have had angel's food, and let your heart return angel's retribution, praise and thanksgiving. If God feeds your bodies, there is none, I hope, such beasts, as will not return the retribution of praises. And will you be slow and backward to it, when he has fed your souls? Shall we bless God for a crumb, and not for a Christ? Other mercies are but crumbs in comparison of this rich mercy, and shall our hearts favor them so much, and not relish these? Other mercies he gives to his enemies, wicked men may run away with the greatest portion of belly-blessings; but these he only bestows on his friends and shall we are unthankful for them? However carnal men are most taken with carnal things; yet sure I am those who are spiritual, as they are most apprehensive of spiritual wants; so the greatest laying out of their spirits in thankfulness is for

spiritual enjoyments. What's corn and wine, *etc.* to this? This is a mercy in which all other mercies are folded up, the *summum genus* of mercy, the top-mercy. God has eminently contain all other comforts; and therefore in the lack of all he can cheer the heart (Hab. 3:7). So Christ does eminently contain all other mercies, and in the want of all, Christ enjoyed, is exceeding great reward. No, all mercies are not only folded up in him, and entailed to him, but he sweetens and sanctifies every mercy. Let us then return home as full of the blessing from on high, so full of praises to the most high. Thankfulness is the great grace to be exercised in, and thankfulness is the great grace to be exercised after; and therefore while the present sense of this mercy warms your hearts, let the heat of it burst forth into thankfulness towards God; it is the most suitable service, and the most suitable time to return it. The best time to have thankfulness in our hearts is when we can look there, and find the mercy for which we praise him also. The best time for praises and thankfulness in our mouths is when we have the blessing in our hands. Well then, all you who are right partakers of this ordinance summon up your hearts to return thankfulness to God. And let your thankfulness carry some proportion with the mercy. The mercy is great, do but measure it in all the dimensions of it: how high? How deep? How broad a mercy? Pardoning, purging mercy, and how long? Even to all eternity; and as the mercy is great, so should be the praises. The more a man's apprehensions are widened to conceive of the vastness and greatness of the mercy, the more will the affections be enlarged to praise him for it. There was never man that did know the preciousness of Christ, and his own need of him, in respect of pardon, purging, and his own unworthiness to partake of so glorious a mercy, but had his heart mightily enlarged to praise God for it. This is that then which God expects at your hands, after he has filled with you the blessing of heaven, that you should return praises to Heaven. Though he does not reap where he does not so we, as that idle servant charged him; yet where God sows blessings, he expects to reap praises. Where there is a flood of mercy, he looks for a stream of thankfulness. O! Then let us proportion our returns to our receipts, let us set up monuments of praise in our hearts and lives for this great mercy; say with David, "Bless the Lord, O my soul," (Psalm 103).

OBEDIENCE AND FRUITFULNESS

2. The second thing required after this ordinance, is obedience, and fruitfulness. That now for the time to come, you should apply your hearts to walk more worthy of God,

unto all manner of pleasing: 1. That we should have our hearts further set against sin; 2. That we should have our hearts further strengthened to service.

1. Get your hearts now further set against sin. O! Let your souls say, "Has God been so gracious, as to renew and confirm my pardon, and shall I again dishonor him? Has he wiped off my former forces, and shall I run on afresh to offend him? Has he taken off my former burden, and cast it on the back of his dear Son, and shall I again lay more load on him? Has he spoken peace to me in his ordinance, and shall I again return to folly? No, far be it from me, I have washed my feet, and how shall I again defile them? I have put off my coat, how shall I again put it on?" says the Christian soul. Profane men, by their sins, as the serpent with his poison, lay it aside when they go to drink, but afterward take it up. Or, as men do with a garment, put it off as at night, but put it on in the morning. And this is fearful, "To return with the dog to the vomit" (2 Pet. 2:22). But God's people cast them away, as a *menstruous* rag, never more to have something to do with them (Isa. 30:22).

2. Get your hearts further strengthened to service. Here is in this ordinance a mutual sealing of Covenants between God and you; as God seals to you, so your seal again to God. God seals to the first part of the Covenant, pardon,

mercy, grace; and you seal to the second part of it, service, subjection, obedience. God gives Christ to you here in this ordinance, and you give yourself back again to Christ. As there is matter of bounty from God to you, so there is matter of duty from you to God; God here in bounty bestows Christ on every humble, broken hearted and believing receiver. They take him, and re-give themselves back again to him for subjection and obedience. There was never any soul, to whom God said in this ordinance, "I am yours," whose hearts did not echo again the same to God, "Lord, I am yours." This head is yours to contrive your glory, this hand is yours to work for you, this heart is yours to love you; he that says, "My beloved is mine," says again, "and I am his," (Song. 2:16). Let us then labor to see our hearts further strengthened to service; let this enable you to walk.

1. More strongly; the sacraments are our spiritual baiting and refreshments which God affords us to strengthen us in our journey to heaven. They are spiritual meat and drink to strengthen us in the performance of all spiritual obedience; such meat as will not only enables a man to work, but to work more strongly. And this to be feared, that they who are never the strongest for service, feed not on the substance, but on shadow, they feed on the elements, but never taste of Christ

the staff of nourishment; and this true here, the meet element is no nourishment.[19]

2. More willingly and cheerfully; Then shall we are able to run the ways of God's Commandments (Psalm 119), when God once here enlarges our hearts. It is said of Jacob, that when he had been refreshed with the preference of God, he plucked up his feet, and went on cheerfully. So here, when the soul has been refreshed with the presence of Christ, he will be able to walk more cheerfully in the ways of God. The food we feed on is angel's food, and will enable us to angel's employments, be to do our work in an angel's spirit, with all alacrity, cheerfulness, joy and delight; though not in the same equality, yet in the same quality, though not in the same measure, yet in the same manner. And so much for the second general, viz. How we must sanctify God in an ordinance.[20]

We will now come to the third general, which is the reason why who ever have something to do with an ordinance of God, must sanctify God in it.

1. *Reason.* Because God commands it. God says he will be sanctified; and Gods will is our law. God does not only command the substance, but the circumstances; not only the matter of worship, but the manner. And though the matter is

---

[19] *Putum elementum non est alimentum*, Psalm 119.
[20] Si quid boni triste

good, if the manner of performance be nothing, God does not regard it. You see what he says to the Jews, "He that sacrificeth, is as he who killed a man, and he that kills a Lamb, as if he cut off a dog's head, and he who burneth incense, as he who blesseth an idol" (Isa. 66:3). These seem strange expressions. What were not these duties as God commanded? Does not *God* command sacrifice, *etc.* Yes, but because they did them not in that manner God commanded, therefore were they abominable to him. If therefore, you give God the bulk of outward performance, without the spirit of devotion; you deal by him, as Prometheus by Jupiter, who ate the flesh and presented him with nothing but bones, covered over with skin; or, to use the Scripture phrase, "you compass God with a lie," (Hos. 11:12). You give him the shell of outward performance, but not the kernel of inward devotion. You give him a body without soul, and as the body without the soul, is dead, and stinks, so does that service which lacks the spirit. As God's will does command service, so our will and affections must perform service. Though our will must be no instrument in performing service. Though God will not own will worship, in regard of prescriptions, yet he will own it in regard of performance, and none else.

So, you see God commands it and therefore, *etc.*

2. *Reason.* Because otherwise we get no good by this ordinance, no good of comfort, nor none of Grace. If indeed the Sacraments did *ex opera operato*, confer grace; or if that this sacrament were an instrument for the begetting of grace in graceless hearts, then might you get good, though you came unprepared.[21] The word, it is set up for that end, to be the instrument of regeneration; and therefore, though you come unprepared close, yet you may be wrought on there. Many that have come to the Word with purpose to scoff, to taunt, to deride; no, to ensnare, and accuse, who yet have been wrought on there, and sent away other men. Were the Sacraments set up for such an end, to beget grace, where there is no grace, then might you get good, though you come unprepared and unsanctified; but as I have told you, it was never set up for such an end. Here it's true, *habenti dabitur*, to him that has shall be given; he that has Grace, shall in the exercise improve his graces; but he that comes graceless goes graceless away; no, worse than he came, which is the next reason.

3. *Reason.* Because otherwise we get much hurt.

The ordinances are not idle, but operative, they either work for *life*, or they work for *death*. As Paul said of the Word, it was *the savor of life, and of death*; so I may say of every

---

[21] *Impii Petram iambunt sed inae necmel ne oleum sagunt* &c. Ambrose *Serm. De caena.*

ordinance. There is never a time you come to hear the Word, but you are set a step nearer heaven, or hell. So never a time you come to receive the sacraments, *etc.* The fruit of the tree of knowledge of good and evil might be wholesome in itself. Yet Adam ate his death when he tasted of it contrary to God's command. So here the sacrament, though in itself it is good, yet it becomes the bane and destruction of those souls, who partake of it unworthily. As the ordinances of God are precious things when God is sanctified in them; so they are costly things, when profaned. Hezekiah knew this full well, and therefore he prays, "Now the good Lord pardon all of those who come to seek the God of their fathers, though they are not prepared according to the preparation of the sanctuary;" he saw the danger of the *unsanctified* use of ordinances.

To be short, it will bring on you, 1. corporal hurt; you see this in the Corinthians, "For this cause many are weak and sickly among you, and many are fallen asleep" (1 Cor. 11:30). It was some epidemical disease, *stagellum inundans*, some overflowing scourge, by which God swept away many in all the quarters of the church; and will you know what was the ground, that was the reason of it? The Apostle tells us that in the beginning, it was for this cause, *viz.*, the profanation, or unsanctified use of this ordinance. There was *mors in olla*, death in the cup, they partook of the cup of the Lord unworthily and drank their own death in it; the cup of life was become a cup of death and the blood of pardon, a cup of guilt.

2. Spiritual hurt, though God does not break out in visible judgments on the carcasses of men as formerly; yet the curse of God eats secretly into the consciences of men. You cause God to give you up to blindness of mind, hardness of heart, and these are curses with a witness; the curse of curses is a hard heart.

3. It puts you in danger of eternal judgment. The Apostle tells you so, "He that eats and drinks unworthily, eats and drinks his own damnation" (1 Cor. 11:29). "Better," says Ambrose, "That a millstone were tied about thy neck, and thou cast into the midst of the sea; than to take the least bit of bread or drop of wine from the Minister, with an unsanctified heart and polluted conscience."[22] And so much for the doctrinal part, we will now come to the application.

APPLICATION OF THE SECOND DOCTRINE

---

[22] *Melius erat mola asinaria colio alligata mergium pelagus quam ulloia conscientia de manu Domini bucellam accipere.* Ambrose, *de caena.*

Use 1. If so, that whosoever has to do with an ordinance, must sanctify God in it; and that there is so much required before, so much in the time, so much afterward, O! How few then shall we find that sanctify God in this ordinance? Some there are who openly profane this ordinance, some who steal a draught of damnation to themselves, your close and civil men; this is the difference, where the common profane man goes to hell the plain road-way, this man steals hell behind the hedge. And indeed, the best of men do not sanctify God as they ought in them. Alas, what preparation before we come on these ordinances? What exciting and stirring up of our graces? What exercise of grace here? Faith, repentance? What thankfulness? What obedience afterwards? Where is the fruit of so many sermons, so many sacraments? Have they not been like rain that falls on the rocks? Are not all these like so many clouds, which pass over our heads, and leave never a drop of moisture behind? Are we not like Pharaoh's lean cow, never the fatter for all our feeding? Are not like men sick of an atrophy, who, though they feed on never so good nourishment, yet they do not grow by it? Do we not shame our meat; discredit those heavenly dainties, that we thrive no more by them? Other ages, like Leah, were bleary-eyed, but fruitful. Ours like Rachel, beautiful, but yet barren. We do not answer God's care and cost towards us; we profit not; we do not grow; and what's the reason? Because we do not sanctify God as we ought in these ordinances; therefore are we so weak in faith, therefore so feeble in grace; therefore corruptions so strong in us. They who look the ordinances should be means for the perfecting of their sanctification; they must labor to sanctify God in them.

Use 2. Is it so? Then it behooves us to enquire, whether we have sanctified God in these ordinances. We have something to do with God's ordinances daily, you see God requires, who ever have something to do with his ordinances, should sanctify God in them. Let us then ask the question of ourselves. Have I sanctified God in this ordinance? I have often come to the sacrament, but have I sanctified God in it? Now you might know this by looking over things. 1. Precedent. 2. Concomitant. 3. Subsequent. But as this time I shall follow this method. Would you know whether you have sanctified God in these ordinances; see then, whether you have observed: 1. God's order, 2. God's rules, and, 3. God's ends; and this before your coming. 2. Whether you have exercised God's graces in the time. 3. Whether you have returned with God's quickening's, God's enlargements, God's enablements afterward.

1. See whether you have observed God's order. Now God's order is this, to justify man, put on him the Wedding

Garment; to sanctify a man, to beget him anew before he bring him on this ordinance. 1. Are you then justified? Has God give you an interest in Christ? Has he discovered your sins to you? Has he humbled your soul under the sense and burden of sin? Has he revealed to you what footing and ground there is in the Word, for receiving graceless persons to life? Has he cleared to you the truth, fullness, freeness, goodness of the promise? Has he brought your soul over to assent to the truth, embrace the goodness, and rest on the firmness of it; and to bring all this home to your own soul? You are a man who is justified, and God calls you close to put his seal to your evidence, that you may be assured forever, that Christ is yours, and you are Christ's.

2. Are you a man sanctified, renewed, regenerated? Has God wrought a thorough, universal, spiritual change? I say spiritual, not a partial, moral, formal change, but a *spiritual*, real, universal change. That you have a new judgment, new will, new affections; where before there was disagreement, now there is a blessed conformity between God and you in all things. You see as God sees, love as God loves; you differ as much from yourself as if another soul lived in the same body, "You were once darkness, now light in the Lord," once dead, now alive, once blind, now see? You are a man whom God calls close to strengthen and nourish his own work in you. As

the maid whom Christ raised from death, he said, "Give her meat;" so Christ having raised you from the death of sin to the life of grace, he calls you close, that you may have meat for the nourishment of spiritual life in you; and this is God's order.

2. You may know whether you have sanctified God in an ordinance, if you examine, whether you have observed God's rules. Now the grand rule is preparation, which lies in two things: examination and excitation of our graces.

1. Examination, "Let a man examine himself, and so let him eat, *etc.*" (1 Cor. 11:28) which examination is more general or more special.

1. More general, of all or our sins; those before, and those after our effectual calling.

2. Of our Graces. 1. What knowledge of God. 2. What faith. 3. What repentance. 4. What love. 5. What hunger and thirst, *etc.*

2. It is more special. 1. How the soul has carried itself under former sacraments, and in particular since the last sacrament; what good it has gotten; what more strength of faith; what more weakening of corruption; what more ability to serve God. And even consider what evil it has done, all which should be set on the soul, with the many aggravations being sins against vows, promises, against covenant, which adds much guilt to sin, and double the offence. 2. The soul is

to examine itself, how it stands for present; what aptness, what fitness for the duty; what sacramental sorrow; what faith to close with God in the present offer, what fitness to join with its fellow members in holy communion and love; what hungering and thirsting after Christ in this ordinance; what spiritual appetite; what present disposition of soul to renew bonds and covenants with God in this ordinance.

Of these and the like are we to examine ourselves; that's the first.

2. There is required excitation of our graces that we stir up our faith, our repentance, our hunger and thirst, *etc.* 1. Our faith to close with a new offer of Christ. 2. Our repentance to mourn afresh. Our hunger and thirst after Christ tendered here. These are God's rules, and if observed, God is sanctified; and that is the second.

3. You may know whether you have sanctified God in this ordinance, if you examine whether you have observed God's ends. Now God's ends are many, *viz.* 1. To glorify God. 2. To get strength against our corruptions. 3. To get increases for our graces. But I shall only name one, set down by the Apostle, "Do this in remembrance of me," (1 Cor. 11:23). Christ did a great work for us, and he is desirous it may not be forgotten; he has taken care it should be remembered both in heaven and in earth. As he remembers it in heaven, it being a part of his

intercession for us there, to represent his blood and sufferings before God. As under the Law, the Priest, when he had offered the sacrifice, was to go with the blood before the Altar and Mercy-seat, and show it to the Lord. So Christ, having offered himself a Sacrifice, presents his blood within the veil, appearing in the presence of God to intercede for us. And as he has taken care to remember it in heaven; so he has taken care to keep it in remembrance on earth (Heb. 9:23). And therefore he has set up this ordinance, to show forth his death, to put us in mind of his sufferings and charges us "to do this in remembrance of him." And when we observe this end truly and rightly as we ought, then do we sanctify God in this ordinance; I say truly and rightly for every remembrance will not serve the turn. 1. It must be cordial and hearty remembrance; we must remember him with an affected heart in Religion (*quod cornon facit, non fit*), what the heart does not do, is not done. Many remember him in a bare historical way; to recount his sorrows, and yet their heart not affected. It is not enough to remember Christ in the head, but you must remember him in the heart; words of knowledge imply affection. It must be cordial. 2. It must be a grateful and thankful remembrance; and there is great cause, it is the top-mercy, that which purchased all for us. Look on all coming swimming in a stream of blood; see on all your mercies engrave. The price of blood, and you will see great cause to be thankful. 3. It must be mourning, bleeding remembrance. So to look on him pierced, as to be pierced; on him wounded, as to be wounded *etc*. And indeed, who can look on Christ in blood, who can behold what he has suffered, and conceive himself to be the actor of all this, and yet the sharer in all the fruit and benefit; for though we were actors of it, ye the put us not out of his *Will and Testament*; he did not except against us in the partaking the fruit of it. Who can so behold him, but must weep over Christ, as the old Prophet over the other, "Alas! My brother! Alas! My brother!" so, "Alas my Christ! Alas my Christ!" 4. It must be a crucifying remembrance; such a remembrance of Christ crucified, as crucifies our sinful affections, our lusts and corruptions, as deals by sin, as sin has dealt by Christ; kills sin, as sin has killed Christ, O! Say, shall I give life to that which has been death of Christ? Shall I cherish that which has killed Christ? Shall I take pleasure in that which has been so bitter to Christ? Shall I count that light and bosom the knife that has killed my Husband? Under the Law, if an ox gored a man, the ox was to die; and shall sin kill Christ, and shall it not die for it? Such a crucifying remembrance it must be, as makes us take up weapons against sin; and he that thus remembers Christ observes God's end, and he who observes God's ends, sanctifies God in his ordinance.

Well then, would you know whether you have sanctified God in this ordinance; see if you have observed God's order, God's rules, God's ends, before you come; and so much for the first.

2. Would you know whether you have sanctified God in this ordinance, see if you have exercised God's graces in the time; what those are, and how to be exercised, I have showed at large.

3. See whether you do return home with God's quickening's, with God's enlargements, with God's enablements? Are you more humble, more serviceable? Are you more thankful? Do you find corruptions weakened, your graces strengthened? Do your endeavors afterward answer your care and conscience before? Is your heart set further against sin? Are the waits of God lovelier to you? Are your souls knit nearer to God, your spirits more inflamed with love of him? These are plain demonstrations that you have sanctified God in this ordinance, and that God has sanctified it to you. But now on the contrary let me tell you: 1. If you have broken God's order and method; that you have come close in a graceless, Christless condition, the soul never yet awakened to see sin, and be humbled for it. You know what

sin is in the Catechism, but do not know what sin is on the conscience; you cannot tell me what faith is in the book, but are not acquainted with the working of it in your soul; and what repentance is, but yet a stranger to it; the day is yet to come in which you set yourself to mourn, and break your heart for sin. Where are the chambers, the closets, the bedsides that can bear witness of your mourning for sin? And yet do you come? You break God's order and so are a profaner of his holy Table. 2. If you break God's rules that do not prepare you by examination and excitation of your graces, but rush into God's presence, breaks in on this ordinance, without any suitable affection to it, you are a profaner of this ordinance, *etc.* 3. If you do not observe God's ends, but come close, as many do; either to avoid scandal, or the censures of men; or, for custom, or for fashion sake, because others come, therefore you will not stay away; or (which I cannot express with abhorrence and detestation enough) because you shall sit at your Master's Table that day, and go into the fields afterward. You are a profaner of this ordinance; and, O! That we had some Tirshatha to drive these away. We read in Ezra 2:61-62 that Tirshatha would not suffer the sons of Kosse and Barzilli to eat of the holy things, because their genealogies were not found registered among them. If you be not in the book of life, if your name be not written in the genealogies of the saints, you are not fit to come.

In the lack of coercive power to fence this ordinance, give me leave to put a few places to you to consider. The first is in Titus 1:15, "To the unclean all is unclean." The second is in Proverbs 21:27, "The prayers of the wicked are abomination." The third, Psalm 66:18, "He that regardeth iniquity in his heart," *etc.* though he never come to act it in this life, "God will not regard his prayers." The fourth, Psalm 50:16, "What hast thou to do, to take my covenant into thy mouth, and hatest to be reformed," *etc.* And if this will not prevail, read and tremble, you profane person, 1 Corinthians 11:29, "He that eateth and drinketh unworthily," *etc.* He is made *guilty* of Christ's death, as Pilate, Herod, Judas, and the soldiers were, he eats and drinks damnation to himself, and for this cause many were sick, weak and fallen asleep; and to this add the example of the unbidden guest, who came without a *Wedding Garment*, if fared ill with them that did not come, but worse with him, which tells us, an unsanctified presence is worse than a profane absence. But yet will you adventure? Do you find anything in the sacrament to encourage you to come? Let us look on it under the several names and notions under which it's presented.

1. It is called a seal, and is the sacrament any encouragement to you under this notion, to whom the Word promises nothing, the sacrament seals nothing? But the Word promises nothing to unregenerate men. All God's Word is against you, nothing for you, and therefore here is but poor encouragement, the seal annexed to a deed, confirms it to none, but such to whom the deed was made. So here, the sacrament being the seal of the Covenant belongs to none, but those to whom the Covenant is made. Now are you out of Covenant, one that has no interest in Christ? You have nothing here.

2. It is called a communion. 1. A communion of the member's one with another. 2. A communion of the members with the head. Now, until you are united to Christ, you have nothing here. Christ derives influence only to branches, life only to his members,[23] he must be in the Son that has life from him. He that has the Son has life, and he that has not the Son has not life.

3. It is called a Supper, the Lord's Supper. Now, is this any encouragement for you to come, who are a profane person?

There are three things requisite in the persons that go to a supper: life, appetite, and apparel.

---

[23] *Qui vult vivere in rapite oportet esse in corpore. Caput corpora sui caput, non alieni.*

1. *Life*: Dead men cannot feed; Christ never spread his Table for dead men. If you are not alive, you are not called to come feed.

2. *Appetite*: What shall they do at a supper that have no stomach, no appetite? And what do you here who have no hunger; no thirsting after Christ, you that never apprehend what lack of Christ, nor never knew the worth of Christ?

3. *Apparel*: No man will go naked to a feast; your apparel here is the Wedding Garment; Christ for justification, Christ for sanctification; and he that came without this, you see what became of him. It would have been better if he had stayed away; it fared better with them than with him. An unsanctified presence will be found as bad as a profane absence. Those that draw near to God in an ordinance, and do not sanctify God in it, God will be sanctified on them.

THE THIRD DOCTRINE

The third and last Doctrine which we now come unto, *viz.*

God will not be sanctified on everyone who does not sanctify him in his ordinances. In the prosecution of which, we will *show*:

1. What is meant by God's sanctifying himself on men.

2. Why God will sanctify himself on those that do not sanctify him in ordinances, and so we shall come to application.

1. For the first, what is meant by God's sanctifying himself on a man.

For the answer of which, I conceive that place which I named in the beginning, Ezekiel 28:22 will afford us some help, "When I have executed my judgments on her, then will I be sanctified in her," on which Jerome said, God is sanctified in the punishment of offenders (*Santificatio Dei est paean pecaniiam*). So you see it in the text, God's punishment of Nadab and Abihu, was the occasion of the word, "I *will* be sanctified."

1. Then God sanctifies himself on men when he inflicts corporal punishments on men for profaning his ordinance. As you see here, and the like, 1 Corinthians 11:29, "For this cause many are sick, *etc.*"

2. God sanctifies himself on men, when he inflicts spiritual punishment on men, *etc. viz.* Security, blindness, hardness, when me do not walk suitably to the light of ordinances, he takes away either light or sight, either ordinances or men's eyes, that seeing they might not see, *etc.*

3. God sanctifies himself on men who profane his ordinance, when he does inflict eternal punishments on men;

this is seen in 1 Corinthians 11:29, "He who eateth and drinketh unworthily, eateth and drinketh damnation to himself;" that which for the present makes him obnoxious to damnation, and shall in the end fix him in the flames, lay him in hell, if he does not repent; yes, and the deepest cellars in hell are for them who have lived in profanation of ordinances. And this in brief shall suffice to tell you what is meant by God's sanctifying himself on men.

REASONS WHY GOD SANCTIFIES HIMSELF

We come to the second thing propounded, what are the *reasons* God sanctifies himself on those that do not sanctify him in ordinances.

1. *In terrorem*, for the terror and dread of all profane persons, that when you hear how God has punished others, who have profaned the ordinances of God, you might tremble, and not dare to profane them. If God should only threaten and should not sometime execute his displeasure on such as were profaners of his ordinances, men would not fear to profane them. They would but make child's play of all the threatening of God, as they did in 2 Peter 3:3, "There shall come in the last day, (ἐμπαῖκται) scoffers," such as shall make child's play of all the threats of God, and look on them but as harmless bug-

bears, to keep them in awe only. But when God does back a threatening with a punishment, as you see he did here in the Text, and on the Corinthians, this strikes dread into the hearts of profane persons.

2. God does it in *cautionem*, for warning. That others παθήματα might be our μαθήματα, others woes, might be our warnings; other sufferings might be standing sermons to us, preaching this lesson, to beware of the like sin, lest you share in the same punishment; therefore God punishes sin in some (*Ne in al os graffetur peccatum*), that other might beware, "And those which remain shall hear and fear, and do no more wickedly," *etc.* (Deut. 29:20). Lots wife was turned into a pillar of salt, to season you, says the Father. Beware of back-sliding. Moses was denied entrance into the Land of Canaan, for his murmuring and unbelief that you might beware. David was punished for his uncleanness, that you might take heed. The man was stoned for gathering of a few sticks on the Sabbath Day, to teach us to beware of profaning the Sabbath. Jerusalem was destroyed for her idolatry, Babylon for her pride, Sodom for uncleanness, the old world for drunkenness, that these might stand up as warnings to us. As the Apostle shows at large, "Let us not be idolaters, as some of them were, *etc.*" (1 Cor. 10:5, 12). All these things happened to them for examples, and admonition to us. We may well say of all, *lege*

exemplum, ne exemplum fias. Read the example, lest you be made an example. Read the example of Pharaoh, destroyed for his oppression, contempt of God, and hardness of heart and beware that you do not the same sins lest God make you an example, *etc.* Read the example of Herod, destroyed for his pride, Jezebel for her paint, Saul for his disobedience; and beware you of the like sin, lest God destroy you. And as in all others, so in this sin of profanation of this ordinance, God does in this way punish the profaners of it, that others might beware of the profanation; therefore he punished the Corinthians with sickness, with death, weakness, for the unworthy partaking of this ordinance, that so they that remained alive, and we that follow them, might beware of the like sin, lest we partake of the like, or a worse punishment; for usually God's second blows are more heavy than the first. They were the first sufferers for their sin; and if they were so heavily punished, what may we then expect, if we do profane this ordinance?

Reason 3. *In manifestationem justifieae.* To declare his justice against sin. God, he made a threatening against this; and if God should not sometimes punish offenders, either men would think they did not offend, or if they did, that God was not just, because he did not punish. Therefore God to clear his justice, and convince men of sin does often sanctify himself on such as profane, *etc.*

4. *Adremovendum scandal;* to take away scandals. As you see does sometime punish his own people, because their sins occasion scandal. God was more dishonored by the uncleanness of David than by all the filth of Sodom; and therefore, because he had caused the name of God to be blasphemed, God punished him, though he pardoned him; and as he does punish his own people, if they sin, because they have given occasion to the wicked, with the Church to blaspheme. So he punishes the wicked, because they give occasion to them, who are without the Church to blaspheme; what will heathens, Turks, and pagans say? Behold what manner of persons they are, who worship this Christ! This is either no Gospel or you are no *Gospellers.*[24]

5. Why God sanctifies himself on such as sanctify him in an ordinance, *is to hold up his great Name and the purity of his ordinances.* God could no way hold up his dread, his fear, his holiness, his glory, his purity and truth of his Word, if God should not punish such as profane his ordinances. You see what a conceit those had of God in Psalm 50:21 because God forbeared to punish offenders: "When thou sawest a thief,

---

[24] *Ecc e quales sunt qui Christum colunt! Aut bacnon est Evangelium, aut vos non est is Evanglici.*

thou consentedst with him, *etc.* These things has thou done and I kept silent." I did not presently come forth to punish you, to execute my judgments on you. And what was the fruit of it? What conceit did this forbearance of God work in those that were guilty? "Thou thought I was altogether such a one as thy self;" that is, that I was one who liked and approved of your doings; you though you did not amiss because I did not punish. Here you see God was wronged by forbearing, and not executing judgment on offenders. And there was no way for God to clear himself, to hold up his great name, but this way, to make them know what they had done, and therefore it follows: "I will set thy sins in order before thine eyes. O! Consider this, ye that forget God, lest, *etc.*" So you see, God does punish offenders, to hold up his great Name, and there is no other way to hold up the name of God, the purity and holiness of God, but by punishment of offenders. You come to the sacrament and you profane this ordinance, God has threatened death and damnation to every unworthy receiver. Why, but you know God does not execute sentence speedily on you, and therefore you think you do not offend, sure God is pleased with it. And therefore God to uphold his name, the purity of his ordinance, and make you know what you have done, sanctifies himself on those who do not sanctify him in this ordinance; sometimes in afflicting visible and corporal judgments on offenders, as you see in the Corinthians; always invisible and spiritual judgments for the present, and eternal judgment if you do not repent. And this you see God does to hold up his name, which otherwise would be polluted by men. As in nature for preservation of the whole, particulars perish. It is better one perish than unity itself. So here, for the preservation of the glory of God (which is worth ten thousand of our lives and souls, as the people said to David) God inflicts punishments on offenders. And there is no other way to preserve or make whole, and repair the honor, glory of God, *etc.* Men that will not learn by the Word must be taught by works; if the Word will not prevail with you, to forbear the profanation of his ordinances, then his works come in. If you will be so sensual and brutish, that you will see nothing to be sin, but what you feel to be sin in God's hand on you, you shall feel blows enough, "A rod is for the back of a fool." Take this with you, whatever you will not learn by faith, you shall be taught by these. God makes men feel those things to be evil by sense, which by faith they would not believe to be evil. When the Word will not prevail with men to forbear profanation of any ordinance, or any sin; then from word he goes to works, lays afflictions, judgments, punishments on men. And happy it is if the works bring men again to the word, when *Scholacrucis* is *Scholalucis*, when God's house of correction is a School of instruction. So says David, "Blessed is the man who thou chastisest, and teachest in thy Law." It was so you see with the Corinthians, the word did not prevail; God goes to his works, inflicts punishments on them, sickness, weakness, death, and then he comes to the word again. "For this cause many are sick." And no doubt, but word on works, was more prevalent with them than when it went alone.

Reason 6. To declare his hatred against sin. God hates all sin; and the nearer a sin comes to God, the more he hates it. Now this is near him, you dishonor his Name; his ordinances are precious, they are his name, and therefore God will not hold such guiltless, *etc.* So you see I have showed you that God will sanctify himself on all those who do not sanctify him in an ordinance. And I have showed you the grounds and reasons of it; now to application.

APPLICATION

Use 1. O! Then take heed you who are a profane person, a swearer, a drunkard, and forbear, unless God make this true of you this day, and raise his glory out of your ruins. You will not be warned by the word, look for works; you whom the examples of others will not make to beware, take heed, unless God do here make you an example. It was the third Captains wisdom in 2 Kings 1:13-14 who, when he saw God's visible judgments went on the two former Captains, he takes warning by it, and avoids their sins; so you that are profane, when you see and hear what God has threatened against profaners of his ordinance; and what fearful judgments God has executed on all unworthy receivers, which are all Christ-less, all graceless persons; O! Beware of coming close in your sins. God's Word is true; as what he promises is sure to come to pass, whatever he threatens. And though he prolongs and defers the time of execution, yet your damnation does not sleep, as Peter says in 2 Pet. 3:7-9, "It shall surely come." If God should threaten to strike dead every unworthy receiver, you would be afraid to come, and how would it make the best of us to look about us, whether we are worthy receivers or not? But alas, what is this threatening in comparison of the other, you eat and drink damnation to yourselves? This is as far above the other as a temporal is below an eternal. A punishment on the body, below the everlasting wrath of God, and punishment of your souls. Better you were struck dead here than reserved for everlasting death hereafter. Your body escapes here (and yet I cannot assure you of that) others, who were God's own people, were struck with death and sickness; and I cannot assure you that God will not destroy you with the bread in your mouth, as he did the Israelites with the quails in theirs. God has threatened, and we do not know whether he will execute, yes, or no. God said, "I will not behold him guiltless that takes my Name in vain." Examples we have; but other examples are worn out, who knows whether he will not give fresh examples, and deal by you as he did by Nadab and Abihu in the text, even in the face with fire from heaven; that all may fear, you went with them, but from fire, to fire, from a destruction by fire, to preservation in fire, from temporal to eternal burnings. But suppose that God should forbear his stroke now, yet it is certain to come. And woe be to them, whose vengeance is reserved for another day. Ah, it will come then with a witness, then with load enough, when the guilt of all your profanations of this glorious ordinance come together; and therefore beware as you love your body; no, your soul and that forever, beware of unworthy partaking's, *etc.*[25]

Use 2. If so, O! Then look to it, you who go on in a way of profanation of God's ordinances. God has said, he will be sanctified of them who draw near to him. And do you believe this? Is it true or is it false? I know you dare not but say this is truth, God himself speaks it. Well then, this being a truth, what may you expect who are a profaner of his ordinances? And to all your profanations, as it was said of Herod, he added

---

[25] *Quorum ultio reponitur in futurum.*

this, that he cast John in prison; so you add this to all the rest, the profanation of his ordinance of the Lord's Supper. O! this is a sin, for which God will not bear with you. If God would not bear with his own people, the Corinthians, who yet had grace, were habitually disposed, were justified, sanctified, and wanted only actual preparation and disposition in the ordinance, how shall he bear with you, you profane person, graceless person? If God deals this way with the green tree, what shall become of the dry tree? If God deals in this way with his own, what shall become of you? If it is this way with the bearing, what shall become of the barren tree? If judgment begin at the house of God, where shall the wicked and sinners appear? Answer me that if you can. If God will be sanctified on his sanctified ones, what of you? If God does punish the want of circumstances, what will he do to you, who lack the substance, the main requisite? But it may be you think there is no such matter, these are but bug-bears, *etc.* For your part, you have come close, and gone home, and found no hurt. And have you so? Bless not yourself in that, there is the more behind. A black and dismal shower of wrath is sure to fall on you one day. This is true; God will be sanctified of them that come nigh him. And this is true also, he who eats and drinks unworthily, is made guilty of the body and blood of Christ; no, he eats and drinks damnation to himself. And this is as true, he who eats and drinks in a Christ-less condition, eats and drinks unworthily. And what do you think will be the consequence of such a sin? Instead of a drinker, you become a shedder of the blood of Christ, as Judas, as Pilate, as Herod. Look on the Jews, and see what it is to be guilty of the body and blood of Christ. It is the heaviest curse in the world, to be guilty of that blood which should save you, pardons you. Shall that which should be a blood of pardon become a blood of guilt? O! What is it to be guilty of that blood that should take away guilt? If you were guilty of all the sins of men on earth, and damned in hell, the blood of Christ could pardon you, and take off that guilt. But what shall take of the guilt of that that should take off guilt? O? See what a sin it is; and in the fear of God, add not this to all your sin, to all your swearing, your profanations, drunkenness, add not this to all, to be guilty of the body and blood of Christ; assure yourselves, God will not care for your bodies, who have no regard to the body of his Son; shall your blood be esteemed, when the blood of Christ is condemned? Shall your lives be prized, when the death of his Son is slighted? No, when you by this shall crucify Christ again? Judge that.

Use 3. Well then, if the sin is so great, and the punishment which God has threatened be so terrible, what care ought we to have, we do not profane this ordinance? And what care to look back into our lives, and see whether we have not profaned this ordinance. The one, to prevent sin not committed, and so to prevent wrath; the other to repent of sin committed, and so to turn away wrath. But you will say, how shall I know whether I have profaned this ordinance? For the answer of which I refer you to what I have said in the second doctrine (where I put the trial on these three *generals*): 1. The observing God's order. 2. God's rules. 3. God's ends. I shall now add three more to help to discover whether you have been profaners of this ordinance, yes or no.

1. When the sacraments work no further good on you, you have profaned this ordinance. I have told you the sacraments are not idle, empty things, but operative, and efficacious toward them who are worthy receivers. Christ cannot be fed on, but he must nourish the soul. A man may feed on other meats and get no nourishment, but he who feeds on this, he finds spiritual nourishment and nourishment. Now then, when men come close and return as empty as they came, as vile as before, there is not fruit can be seen in their lives and conversations; here a man may suspect the ordinance is profaned. When men were filthy, and are filthy still, swearers, and are so still; drunkards and remain so still; this is an evident demonstration you have been a profaner of this ordinance. Indeed God's people do not ever get the good they

expect, never get the good they desire. But yet some good is gotten, some more strength of grace, some more working out of lust, although for the present they cannot apprehend it. But the other now, they get none; they come graceless to it and go graceless away. And it must necessarily be so, this is no ordinance for the working of grace, in graceless persons, but for the nourishing of grace in those whom God has wrought grace in, as I have showed at large.

So that is the first, when we get no good.

2. When a man is worse after than before, this is an evident sign he has profaned this ordinance. When a man is strengthened in a state of sin returns with more violence to any particular sin; as you see Judas, the Devil entered into him, he took fuller and stronger possession of him; and you shall see the ordinary fruit of profanation of this ordinance, men wax worse and worse, proceeding from evil to evil. It may be, when first they came to receive, they were fearful; for there is some natural tenderness of conscience in men, and they are afraid to come to so great an ordinance, without some kind of preparation; and therefore it may be they did catch up a book the day before, and say prayers more, carry themselves demurely. But afterwards, when men are grown up in the profanation of this ordinance, they can look on all the threats, on all the judgments denounce against them, never tremble.

And what is the reason they tremble before, and do not now? Their condition never the better it may be far worse. Why, here is the reason, the custom of profanation of this ordinance, has hardened them in their way, they now fear nothing, their heart is fortified. They have sinned away those common principles, that natural tenderness, that was once in them. Sin is an eating thing, it eats out the very heart of everything which is good in men. A man may not only sin away his moral principles, but he may sin away the very principles of nature. Sin will never leave, until it has made all as vile as itself (Rom. 1:26-27). When men live in the profanation of this ordinance, they wax worse and worse. That man runs violently on in sin, who sets out from the profanation of God's ordinance, because he runs with the Devil's strength. Satan has filled his heart with more mischief. As the saints run more actively in the ways of God after, so the wicked more violently in a way of sin. The profanation of this ordinance strengthens men to further sin; either as 1. One sin disposes a man to another, helps the birth of another.

2. No, and one sin strengthens a man to the commission of another. As one duty of godliness does dispose and enable to the performance is another. So one sin disposes and strengthens to the commission of another. The sin of unworthy eating does strengthen to more sin; such a man, he

gets more heart to sin. He that dares break through threatening here to sin will not stick to do it in other cases. It causes God to give us up to blindness of mind, hardness of heart, *etc.*, which gives Satan further footing in men's hearts, to egg them on to all manner of wickedness. You see it in Judas; and therefore, if you find yourself worse in life and conversation, there's a manifest sign you have profaned this ordinance.

3. When a man feeds on nothing, but the outward element, the bread and wine, and not on Christ in the promise, he profanes this ordinance. If you do not feed on *panem Christum*, as well as *panem Christi*, the bread which is the Lord, as well as the Bread of the Lord, you profane this ordinance. A man may eat bread and drink wine in an ordinary way and not sin; but he who eats Bread and drinks Wine in the way of an ordinance, and does not feed on Christ himself, he is a profaner of this ordinance. Now you cannot feed on Christ in a sacrament, until you have fed on Christ in a promise. You cannot feed on Christ sacramentally until you first feed on Christ spiritually. And have you ever fed on Christ in the promise? Did ever God discover sin to you, and humble your soul for it? Did ever God reveal Christ to you and bring your heart to close with him? Then you have fed on Christ, and may come. But he who never fed on Christ

spiritually can never taste him sacramentally. You have no organ, no eye of faith to see Christ here, nor no mouth of faith to taste him here, no life to desire him, and therefore cannot feed on him. And he who does not feed on Christ here is a profaner of this ordinance. A man may feed on Christ and never taste of the bread and wine and yet have the same benefits (John 6:53). A place which is spoken of the spiritual feeding on Christ, out of the use of the sacrament. But a man cannot feed on the bread and wine and not feed on Christ, but he profanes this ordinance. Christ without these may be fed on, but not these without Christ. If your body feed on these, and your soul does not feed on Christ, you are a profaner of this ordinance. Well then, to sum up all in this; would you know whether you have profaned this ordinance?

1. See if you have observed God's order, *etc.* If you have not observed God's order, that you come close in a Christless, graceless condition, unjustified, and unsanctified; lacks your faith; lacks your repentance; lacks your hunger and thirst; lacks your knowledge? You are a profaner of it. And alas, of that literal trial I have had in this last matter, *viz.* knowledge, I have found great lack. You would admire if I should tell you the senseless answers I have had; I do not speak of all, there are some who are but green in years, yet are ripe in knowledge; but yet may who are grace in years extreme

ignorant. Ask them what a sacrament is, they cannot tell; ask them for what end they come to the sacrament, they tell me to nourish their bodies; what God requires they do not know. And such answers, that a man might have as much comfort to give the sacrament of the Lord's Supper to a child, as to such ignorant creatures. I am sure there is less sin in one, than the other, and there is not much more knowledge. It is true indeed, if a man had never so much knowledge, if he could tell me as much as any in the world, of the nature of God, of Christ, of the sacraments, *etc.*, yet without grace this would not make him a worthy receiver. The devil knows more than most men, for the speculative part; yet what is he the better for that? But yet if a man is ignorant, he must needs be a profaner of the ordinance. A man may have knowledge, and yet not have grace, but if he have no knowledge, he is certainly graceless. So the wise man says, "Without knowledge, the mind is not good." We have a profane Proverb, "He that made us, save us." But God answer that in Isaiah 27:11, "Ye are a people of no understanding, therefore he that made you will not save you, and he that formed you will show no mercy on you." And he threatens in 2 Thess. 1:8, "To come in flaming fire, taking vengeance on them that know not God, and that obey not the Gospel of Christ." And therefore beware you who are ignorant persons, of coming, you will profane this ordinance. And you who are graceless persons, though you should know as much as all the men in the world, do not come here, if you do, you break God's order, and so profane this ordinance. 2. If you have not observed God's rule, examined yourself, and excited and stirred up your graces.

3. If you have not observed God's ends, *etc.* you will be profaners of this ordinance of God. And I think this should terrify you, who are profane persons; sure you have reason in you, though you want grace. Do you hear what God says, he will be sanctified in them that come near him? Have you not heard, he that eats and drinks unworthily is made guilty of the body and blood of Christ? Does not God say that whoever eats and drinks unworthily, eats and drinks damnation to himself? And have not I cleared to you, all Christless, graceless persons are unworthy receivers? And yet will you come? Beware, lest God show some visible judgment on you; beware lest God teach you by works, who will not lean by word. See what befell Nadab and Abihu here, because they did not sanctify God. Read what befell the Corinthians; read what befell the man in the Gospel, who came without his wedding garment, "Take him hence and cast him into utter darkness, *etc.*" Let former examples move you, lest God make you an example (*Lege exen plum, ne exemplum fias.*). Think, God is the same God still, his glory as dear to him, his ordinances as precious. As he

is the same towards the saints in the ways of mercy, so you may expect him the same to you in the ways of judgment; and if this does not move you, if this will not persuade with you to forbear, I wash my hands of the guilt of the blood of your soul, I have given you warning, and your blood is on your own head; and I wish the guilt of the blood of Christ is not on you too. Let me then beseech you, in the bowels of love and compassion, as you love your souls, as you love your bodies, as you would not be guilty of your own blood. No, as you would not be guilty of the blood of Christ; as you would not eat and drink damnation to yourselves; as you would not provoke God to break in on you, and inflict his severe judgments on you, come not here. Do not come here, you ignorant person, you graceless, Christless person, you swearer, you drunkard, you covetous person; no, come not here, whoever you are, who are servants to any lust, who live in any known sin, lest God make this good on you, which I have preached to you. That because you do not sanctify God in this ordinance, he will sanctify himself on you; because you do not glorify him, he will raise his glory out of your ruins. But while I speak thus sadly to the bad, let me not be a terror to the good. I would not break the bruised reed, nor quench the smoking flax. As I would not give encouragement to graceless persons, so I would not discourage the least work of grace in any. As I would not cherish any false fire, unfound work, so I would not quench any spark of God's kindling. Have you some work of God on your spirit? Has God discovered to you sin and misery? Has he humbled you for it? Has God revealed Christ to you, stirred your heart with desires after him, that riche without Christ, relations, comforts, the world without Christ will not satisfy you. All these are like a feast without an appetite, a paradise without a Tree of Life, too low either for you to feed on, or to find comfort and satisfaction in them; do you seek after Christ, pursue Christ; do you cast yourself in his arms to save, at his feet to serve? Why, such I would invite, "Ho, everyone that thirsteth, come to the waters" (Isa. 55:1); here close with Christ, feed on Christ; and to such I would say, Christ is properly and truly food for your souls; and feeding on him, your souls shall live, in grace here, in glory hereafter.

FINIS